CORPORATE
INNERVATION

UNLOCKING THE GENIUS
INSIDE YOUR ORGANISATION

ALLY MULLER

'Ally has created an inspiring roadmap for innovation and has supported the teams through the development and implementation of a transformative innovation framework. Ally engaged all staff from the leadership team to the employees on the ground and provided the space, tools and guidance to develop an inclusive portfolio of ideas and coached the teams from idea genesis to implementation. She has implemented a human-centric framework that has shifted our view of innovation that is driving the right ideas for the business.'

Krishan Tangri, Executive General Manager Infrastructure Development and Delivery, Brisbane Airport Corporation

'Ally is a fiercely independent thinker yet exhibits an unwavering commitment to collaborate. As a bold leader Ally enables and promotes discussion and can align strategies with the required pace of any organisation.

As a keen futurist Ally can show an alternative path and what could be, while working on the very foundations required. As an agent of change Ally generates enthusiasm and optimism throughout an organisation through her passion and infectious disposition.

Ally is the catalytic converter our organisation needed. I have no doubt yours too.'

Dave G. Whimpey, CEO, Surf Lifesaving Queensland

'The area of innovation has seen a recent surge in terms of people providing consultancy. However, very few possess the drive required to succeed. Even fewer understand the organisational context and the contrasting nature of innovation itself for each organisation. This is where Ally differentiates herself from the rest of the pack.

From an organisation standpoint, innovation and ideas are always there. People within the organisation have always had them. But they are being impeded by organisational processes and culture. To nurture someone else's idea, remove organisational roadblocks and create organisational acceptance is not an easy task. Above it all, to create a process that encourages innovation and embed it in the organisational culture is the true challenge. This is where Ally succeeds within the innovation space.'

Shoaib Mulla, Strategic Portfolio Office, Brisbane Airport Corporation

'I had the pleasure of working with Ally and initially I was a bit sceptical when she presented a proposal to establish an innovation process that will change the way (culture) we currently work in our Asset Management Group. My scepticism was based on comparing our prevailing innovative culture to the Corporate Innervation framework and thought it was a bit far-fetched. I very quickly realised that what I know about innovation and developing new ideas against the approach she applied, are miles apart. Ally is a subject matter expert who can solicit, plan and implement innovative ideas from bottom up and apply mandates and governance downwards without losing creativity and assertiveness. Good value for companies who want to make innovation a part of their strategy and implementation plan. I am really impressed!'

Robbie Pretorius, Principle – Services Lead, SNC Lavalin

'The word innovation is used and overused a great deal, particularly in challenging times. I just love the way Ally Muller has taken a long, hard look at innovation and shown us what we are missing. Through her work, her powerful framework and her depth of experience, Ally will have a lot of high level executives asking themselves what exactly does innovation really mean to them and to their organisations.'

Andrew Griffiths, International Bestselling Business Author, Global Speaker

'Ally Muller is a powerhouse of skill and expertise when it comes to elevating businesses to the next level. Her thirst for knowledge and impeccable application of enterprise innovation principles, with a steady foundation in corporate finance and strategy is what sets her apart from the rest. Ally is a unique thinker with a pragmatic baseline. With presence as a board member for a number of organisations which contribute to shaping the next generation, her contribution to the community and business landscape in Australia will be felt for many years to come.'

Crystal Evans, Head of People and Culture, Surf Life Saving Qld

For Elise

Acknowledgements

Thank you to everyone who has supported me in writing this book. All the love, support, coffee, laughter and childcare has been greatly appreciated. Particularly the never-ending belief in me. With special thanks to my Mum, my love Steve and Crystal.

Special thanks to Andrew Griffiths for believing in me, my framework and providing me with guidance, support and laughter throughout the writing of this book. Your insights and knowledge have been invaluable in this process.

And lastly, my beautiful daughter Elise, thank you for inspiring me to always strive for more.

First published in 2020 by Ally Muller

© Ally Muller 2020
www.allymuller.com
www.goyaconsulting.com.au

A catalogue entry for this book is available from the National Library of Australia.

ISBN: 978-1-922391-04-9

Printed in Australia by McPherson's Printing

Project management and text design by Publish Central

Cover design by Peter Reardon

Author photo by Olessia McGregor

The paper this book is printed on is certified as environmentally friendly.

Contents

Introduction

Do you want your organisation to endure over decades and not just a short period of time? This will require an ability to create value, evolve and innovate in a way that develops creative opportunities which provide revenue and benefits to the whole organisation.

Corporate longevity is rapidly declining. In 1958 listed companies had an estimated lifespan of 60 years, and today the average lifespan of a listed company is less than 18 years. A number of different forecasts show this lifespan will decline to 12 years by 2027. For some of you, 2027 will be in your current long-term strategy. Have you thought about this?

Do you want to stay relevant today or increase your longevity in the marketplace? Or both? These are the tough questions leaders and strategists need to be asking themselves every day.

There are many reasons why organisations go into decline, or meet their demise, and these will vary from being acquired, mergers, being overtaken by faster growing companies, or simply holding onto old, tired business models that are fading. Sometimes this happens slowly, and other times it happens fast. Faster than we thought possible because of new technology, economic externalities or an aggressive competitor we didn't see coming.

RETHINKING CORPORATE INNOVATION

Let's be honest – we've all been 'innovated' up the wazoo. Everything from using Zoom to work from home to the development of artificial intelligence solutions and everything in between has been referred to as 'innovation'. It seems we want our organisations to be innovative, but for so many we've lost the meaning and concept of what this really is. It's time to rethink innovation in the corporate environment, and incorporate it as a human-centric process focused on building a culture for the long game. One that becomes self-sustaining and lasts well beyond the tenure of the current leadership team. What a legacy that would be for these leaders. Who doesn't want that?

Innovation is a huge opportunity in the corporate world, but many organisations are missing the boat by shackling themselves to a hustle culture and startup mentality that doesn't easily align inside the corporate environment. We really want to innovate, but it seems just out of reach.

I have studied extensively the state of innovation and the results occurring at a macro and micro level. I have spent countless hours talking with boards and executive teams to support their vision for innovation, and guide them with the challenges they are having translating this vision into bottom-line value.

Spoiler alert: it's not about disruption or creating the next 'unicorn'. I shift their focus to their people – their greatest asset, biggest source of functional ideas, and the weapon against disruption from the startups and competitors so many leadership teams are worried about.

I work with boards and executive teams in organisations ranging from large multinational conglomerates to not-for-profits, and I see the same problems time and again to do with innovation. The intentions are good, but more often than not, the strategy and leaders are not focusing on the right solutions, inhibiting the organisation's ability to truly build an innovation portfolio that adds value. It's time to rip the 'theatre of innovation' out of the organisation and kick it to the curb. It's not about matching T-shirts, ping-pong tables, or even the funkiest new tech (that someone else made). I show my clients how to create a 'Corporate Innervation Operating System' that builds a human-centred process and culture which adds value to their bottom line.

THE GOOD, THE BAD, AND THE UGLY

What I have done in this book is a warts-and-all review of corporate innovation – the good, the bad and the ugly – to show you where I see organisations tripping up and hampering their ability to deliver on their innovation goals. I have unpacked the demons of innovation to talk about why innovation programs fail or don't deliver the intended, or any, value to the bottom line. This is not to name and shame any bad behaviours, rather it's to call out the patterns, myths and theatre that we all fall into. We want to get better together, so we need to confront these hard issues head on to remove them from the organisation. Then I am going to introduce you to my nine-step framework for Corporate Innervation which you can implement immediately in your organisation.

To get the most out of this book, I want you to open your mind to rethinking how you are going to deliver innovation inside your organisation. Forget about how you are already doing it and, most importantly, remove the startup, hustle culture and style of working from your process. You're not a startup. It's unlikely you'll have the appetite for the failure rates and years of expenditure without income for each idea. You're a large organisation, with bureaucracy, processes, shareholders, and revenue and performance targets you are required to meet. You need to do it differently. It needs to be smart, inclusive and open to the right type of ideas for growth.

A HUMAN-CENTRED APPROACH TO INNOVATION

As you read this book, I hope you will create a vision for an inclusive, human-centred approach to innovation inside your organisation. This is not about perfection, nor is it a competition for which organisation has the best innovation program. My goal is to share with you the techniques, solutions and processes that have provided the greatest returns for myself and my clients over many years. It's too easy to get caught up in spending all our time in the 'busyness' of work. I want you to have an easy-to-use framework that will deliver value, now and into the future.

You will notice a number of stories from movies, their production and the rationale of their creative process, and this is not just because I am a bit of a cinephile, it's because I am in the middle of an exciting new project and it's front of mind for me. I am using my own principles and working with a number of executive producers and directors to build an innovative film-funding vehicle to finance and produce more films in Australia. I really do walk my own talk and use this framework in my own business to build innovative business models. Because it works!

If you're seeking a better way to manage innovation inside your organisation, with a portfolio of ideas that will deliver real bottom-line value, this is the framework for you. Yes, this will take time, leadership and dedication to building a human-centric innovation framework. This is more than just creating innovative products and solutions to make more money. This is about the longevity and culture of your organisation and making a solid return on your investment in innovation.

What could possibly be a better investment in your organisation than that?

THE FUNDAMENTALS OF CORPORATE INNERVATION

Before we go any further, here are my core fundamental principles of 'Corporate Innervation'. Corporate Innervation is a human-centric business model that changes the rules of innovation by removing the complex, focusing on value and developing the greatest asset – your people. As we go through this journey together I want you to think about how you can implement these principles in your organisation:

1. **Everyone has a role to play in innovation.** It's the job of everyone inside the organisation.

2. **Get comfortable being uncomfortable.** Innovation is uncomfortable, messy and unpredictable. If you're not uncomfortable, you're probably not doing it right.

3. **Innovation is more than a product, service or visionary dream.** Innovation is a community inside your organisation. A community of culture that's passionate, persistent, collaborative, knowledge seeking and inclusive.

4. **Innovation isn't an extracurricular activity** – it's a core part of your business rhythm. Create the space, time and resources to make it happen.

5. **Fall in love with the process!** Ideas are cheap, fast and easy, but it takes time, persistence and dedicated people to bring ideas to life.

6. **Innovation is an attitude** that's almost impossible to achieve through process alone.

7. **The genius is in your people.** Give them a voice. They see the problems, challenges and opportunities that others walk past every day.

8. **Don't be distracted by disruption.** Disruption is born out of customer dissatisfaction or not solving one of their problems. Fall in love with your customers and give them what they need so that you're not distracted by disruption – it's very hard to disrupt an organisation that is fulfilling the needs of their customers and they are happy.

9. **Ideas and employees are the heroes** of your innovation framework, and your innovation leaders are their guides.

10. **Success is a repeatable, scalable and pervasive innovation process and culture in your organisation.** It's not a one-hit wonder or lucky break.

There will never be a better time to build a Corporate Innervation Operating System to grow the value of your people and the bottom line. I'm all in!

Join me and let's have some fun.

PART I

What *is* Corporate Innervation?

SO WHAT *IS* CORPORATE INNERVATION? It is a culture, a lifestyle, a way of thinking and holistic belief that your people are your innovation assets and the activation of the framework will support the development of a perpetual and self-sustaining innervation system inside an organisation. This is a mindset, coupled with a framework to shift an entire organisation to growth through innovation.

Corporate Innervation as a culture and process was born through my time consulting with boards, executive teams and innovation leaders, because they often developed and implemented strategies that suggested they felt immune to creative destruction and their demise in the marketplace. No organisation is immune to this, nor will one or two great ideas save an organisation that is already in trouble. Innovation is too often focused on the desire to be the disrupter, and leaves the organisation, customer and focus on growth in the dust. Why? Well, there are many reasons for this, but the most important are hubris and certainty in their ability to strategise, innovate, and decide the future in a bubble.

As an outside consultant looking in, I see this play out on a daily basis, through the replication of strategies which worked in the past or those that have been lifted and shifted from other organisations, whether that be through the movement of staff between organisations or consultants providing their standardised frameworks. True innovation is always the poor cousin in these instances, and often I see people wanting their business to be something it is not and probably never will be: an earth-shattering, disruptive startup that is the newest and sexiest unicorn. These are the dreams of actual startups, and not the corporate innovation dreams we should be aspiring to.

I feel like in theory everybody gets this. It makes perfect sense. But when this is translated into a program of work, there is a distinct shift from what would create an inclusive and self-sustaining innovation portfolio to what actually happens. There is still a huge emphasis on external programs and ideas that are more theatre than value adding. And let's not forget about funding – innovation programs are generally unfunded and under-resourced.

How can organisations want innovation so much, yet they don't give it the love and respect it deserves? You can't get something from nothing, and your employees know this and will treat your innovation program accordingly.

Innovation, innovation and more innovation. It seems that everybody and everything wants to be innovative. Almost 90% of organisations have 'innovation' in their values, strategy or aspirations.[1] We are obsessed with being innovative. Innovation and its importance in the market are nothing new, but the attention we are placing on innovation is creating a crazy and chaotic view.

You're not a startup, so stop behaving like one. You don't need to be disruptive. Being disruptive shouldn't be the aim of your corporate innovation program. If you are only focused on disruption there's an excellent chance you'll cannibalise a section of your business, which can be very destructive to the organisation overall. Or in the case of Yahoo, can lead to the significant decline and the path to death of an organisation. Once, Yahoo was the leader of the pack in the search engine market, but this position was lost to Google, and then they were shifted into third by Microsoft's Bing. The CEO at the time, Marissa Mayer, was focused on the premise that technology was disrupting their business. The thought was that the abundance of startups in this area was disrupting them, and if the valuations were low enough they could buy these potential threats to maintain and grow their position. A plan was hatched and Yahoo went shopping.

By 2016, Yahoo were reported to have spent between US$2.3 billion and US$2.8 billion to acquire 53 tech startups. Now this was a sensational payday for many of the startups that were acquired, but maybe not a great strategy for Yahoo. Over time, Yahoo shut down 33 of these newly acquired startups, discontinued the products of a further 11,

---

1   Global Innovation Index.

left seven to their own devices, and integrated two of their acquisitions, Tumblr and BrightRoll.

The intense focus on disruption and removing their potential competitors from the market stopped Yahoo from seeing the bigger picture. Disruption isn't driven by technology. It's born out of customer dissatisfaction of not solving one of their problems. Success should be driven by value to the customer and not to the organisation. Don't you want to make collaborative experiences and extensions of your current products?

The acquisition strategy Yahoo used inhibited their growth, and in 2017 it was acquired by Verizon for less than US$5 billion, which was a long way down from the peak of its valuation of US$100 billion. What Yahoo failed to understand is that disruption is a customer-driven process and consumers will be attracted to a better and more efficient customer experience. Most times the technology of the disrupter isn't better or more innovative, it's just that they've understood the pain points or the holes in the market better and are able to provide the customer exactly what they want.

For innovation to work in the corporate environment, we need to fight for the customer experience and not against it. The focus needs to be on doing the little things every day that improve the customer experience. We want to grow and work with our customers. The reason new players and disrupters can come into the market is they enter by taking the experience or activities the customers are not happy with and filling the gap with their product or service.

Disruption is interesting, but don't let it be your driver for innovation. Make your customer the hero and give them what they need.

Here's my one and only Steve Jobs reference. Jobs wasn't interested in disrupting the industry. He wanted to create an exceptional and beautiful customer experience. He grew an abundant market. He didn't kill it.

Disruption doesn't create an abundant and infinite mindset for growth. It doesn't raise and develop the skills of the people inside the organisation. It doesn't feed the ecosystem of innovation for growth – it starves it of oxygen.

It seems we want the dream of innovation but are unsure of how to really make this work. In my conversations with boards, CEOs and strategy executives, the rationale varies from seeking to attract and retain talented employees, seeking relevance and a competitive advantage to enhancing the offer to customers. The intentions are usually focused on creating value. So why does it generally go astray and end up not delivering what we want it to?

We have blurred the lines between the startup culture and building a culture of innovation that will deliver value inside an organisation. The hype and hustle culture and startup fanfare have caused many organisations to take their eye off the ball and focus on the wrong things.

There's an abundance of software, ways of working and other 'tools' available in the market for organisations to implement. Many of them are fabulous, and you can find one that will suit your organisation. But they will not make your organisation innovative, they will not come up with the ideas and they won't create a culture of growth and innovation. They will help your workflow and collaboration process, but without the ideas, culture and people, they are worthless. You need that secret sauce and culture to make it work, because a hammer won't build a house for you. You need a team of skilled people, the tools, and a set of plans that everyone is working from to bring the design to life and make it a structure that lasts. You want this to be something that lasts beyond the cycle of your employees.

Innovation happens at all levels of the organisation. This is fabulous rhetoric I hear leaders spruik all the time, but very rarely do I see this in action. I realised that it wasn't through the leaders not wanting to deliver on this promise, rather it is through an inability to actively engage all members of an organisation to understand and participate in the vision of innovation. It is not enough to set aside a team of people to innovate. Leaders need to make space for all employees to be actively engaged in the culture of innovation through guiding, coaching and mentoring the development of their ideas.

I'm a passionate entrepreneur who's managed to grow and sell a number of businesses, a finance nerd, and I am extremely passionate about the customer experience. It's the combination of these three passions that led me to develop the Corporate Innervation Operating System. It was born out of frustration at the continual desire of many organisations to look for outside 'wisdom and genius' to hand them the golden ticket for innovation. Most times it was actually sitting right there in front of them, but they couldn't see it. In a nutshell, the Corporate Innervation Operating System has been designed to do two things:

- humanise the innovation process to unlock the existing genius inside your organisation to build a future-proof culture of growth

- monetise innovation to add value to the bottom line.

I hope this book will cause you to reflect on the way you view innovation inside your organisation and seek a different way of doing things. This is going to be a journey that's both fun and a little confrontational. We need to clean out the bad habits, myths and mistakes to develop a functional Corporate Innervation process that will really add value to your organisation.

Why we do innovation will determine *how* it is done and the outcomes achieved. I am going to ask you to:

- rethink your vision and purpose for innovation – to change from what you think you should do and transform into a vision for longevity and growth built on a process of sustainable innovation

- understand your people are the genius inside your organisation and you need to unlock and harness their ideas, because they have knowledge, experience and wisdom

- create an inclusive culture of Corporate Innervation that becomes self-sustaining, beyond the current leadership team, to drive the organisation forward

- future-proof your organisation by consistently leading with the needs of your customers, internal and external, to build a structured innovation program to support the organisation to weather external shocks, disruptions and aggressive competition.

It's time to really dig deep and rethink how you view innovation inside your organisation. My vision is to change the way organisations approach innovation. It will require the utilisation of everyone inside the organisation, and the ability to harness their collective wisdom that will create new products to protect against disruption and dissatisfied customers, uncover the blindspots that can weaken your position, and create longevity in the market.

What do we really mean when we talk about 'innovation'?

Innovation needs to be a systematic, integrated ecosystem that everyone in the organisation participates in.

Innovation is exciting, transformative and often can be a key driver of growth in an organisation. But for many organisations it's still seen as a 'nice to have', as opposed to an imperative program of work. They want to put innovation up in lights as one of their values, aspirations and a key component of their strategic agenda, but it's unfunded, under-resourced and often unable to be delivered upon.

At the executive and board table, there is usually a strong focus on innovation to be a core component of any strategy. These conversations are robust and intended to stimulate the growth of innovation ideas, portfolios and future advantages in the market. I know, because as a board member I drive this agenda, and I work with the boards and executive teams of my clients to embed a structured innovation ecosystem that will continuously add value to the bottom line.

THE STATE OF PLAY FOR CORPORATE INNOVATION

More than three-quarters of organisations aspire to have 'innovation' as a corporate value. When I discuss this with my clients, there are some common themes on their rational for this:

- seeking new avenues for growth through the development of something 'new' that will add value to the organisation
- development of a high-performance culture
- attracting talent through becoming an employer of choice.

But, what does it *really* mean? Well, that depends on the organisation, their leadership and the direction the board is driving them in. The intent is often the same, but the energy, focus and weight put behind it in terms of budget and resources will determine the seriousness of the leadership team to embed innovation in their organisation.

Corporate innovation is certainly a key focus for what appears to be most organisations. It's in their vision, values, and if you take a look at an org chart you are highly likely to find a number of senior and executive people who have 'innovation' in their title. So it seems most organisations want to be innovative and create transformative and breakthrough opportunities, but are they really effective at doing so?

The data suggests that these goals are aspirational, and the maturity of this process is very low, and perhaps ad-hoc for most.

In a 2019 KPMG study of corporate innovation, researchers spoke to 215 professionals with a remit that includes innovation, strategy and R&D and asked them to assess their innovation programs in terms of maturity and the impact provided for the organisation. Over 77% of the people participating in the survey were director, executive and C-suite level in their organisation.

Interestingly, only 12.8% of respondents reported a high level of maturity for corporate innovation, stating they had an integrated innovation program organised with systems and processes and an innovation portfolio that is tied to the corporate vision with formal links to funding projects. Of this, 1.9% (or four organisations) described themselves as having the 'nirvana' of innovation programs that is scalable, repeatable and pervasive – it's part of their corporate DNA. In these organisations, the executives told the researchers that innovation is the responsibility of all departments, functions and employees in the organisation.

These figures tell a very bleak story for corporate innovation. This shows that while there is a lot of talk about corporate innovation and aspirations in this area, a significant amount of work needs to be done to get there. The KPMG survey found that while 100% of respondents were focused on innovation, their efforts were still tiny, unfocused, and did not have an ecosystem or structure to organise and develop proof of innovation in the organisation.

Why don't most organisations get there? The answers were very clear: the barriers to success seemed to come down to the culture and leadership of the organisation struggling with the soft challenges of culture and creating alignment between business units, and the hard challenges of understanding failure and knowing that not every project will deliver value or tangible results. The other reported key barriers to an integrated innovation program were:

- turf wars
- competing priorities
- little or no budget
- no vision for innovation
- not aligned with the rest of the business
- culture clashes
- searching for the unicorn.

It appears the desire is there, but the actions to enable successful corporate innovation are not.

RETHINKING CORPORATE INNOVATION

When I talk to my clients about corporate innovation I tend to initially hear all the trendy buzzwords around agile teams, new ways of working, hackathons, pitch fests … you pick the term and they will talk to me about it. Often there is also a mindset that innovation must be a transformational digital offering. It seems like innovation is becoming one of those cringe-worthy, overused terms like 'synergies', 'move the needle', 'disruption', 'pivot' … I could go on, but I think you get the picture.

Innovation is a discipline, and it's nothing new. Innovation is the management of the development of a new idea from genesis, throughout its entire lifecycle, and into the end of its life. Innovation is often confused with creativity, but that is merely idea generation. Business disruption and continuous reinvention are also nothing new, so I find it disturbing when this is referred to as 'the new normal'.

The role in innovation by employees in business has been around for longer than we have referred to it as innovation. An incredible example of this, and one that has truly stood the test of time, is the invention and implementation of a cork fixed with a wire cage – a 'muselet' – as an effective stopper for champagne, allowing it to ferment in the bottle. Invented in the 1690s, this is something that champagne houses and makers of sparkling wine use around the world to this day.

The story is a fascinating one, and one that is steeped in the need to solve a business problem, which was seeking a slower fermentation of the wine in the bottle which was held in place with wooden bungs and hemp string, in order to create a clearer and more bubbly sparkling wine. The Abbey that ran the vineyard in question was struggling financially due to years of wars, invasions and a number of poor crops. They desperately needed to think of a way to enhance their wine and increase sales, if only to support the Abbey. Dom Perignon experimented with cork and wire cages to hold the cork in place, and while there were a number of iterations over time to get it right, what you see today is similar to the final design used in the 1700s.

While there were many things that Dom Perignon did to create the start of the legacy of this champagne house, he wasn't focused on disrupting the market. He was focused on the creation of value in the market in order to enhance and grow the market.

The point about this isn't just that it's incredible that something we almost don't even notice when we open a bottle of champagne was created in the 1690s to support a vineyard's ability to create a more bubbly, clear sparkling wine, and to enhance sales. The genius was inside the vineyard in the form of Dom Perignon and his team, and the innovative solution came about through their experimentation and determination to find a way to ferment a better wine and sell more to keep their Abbey in the black.

While innovations and incredible new ideas can happen by chance, the reality is that today they most often take place inside a complex and bureaucratic organisational system, and we have been looking at it in a bit of a topsy turvy manner. Fundamentally, innovations occur because we are solving a problem; we want to do something better or we believe there is something missing in a process.

There is a misconception that innovation is a sexy, dark and mysterious process that creates market-disrupting or transformational change, always with the secret dream of being the next unicorn that creates a multi-billion-dollar platform. That's an impressive aspiration, but that's not what corporate innovation is likely to achieve. Multi-billion-dollar successes are extremely rare – not impossible, but rare. As such, the focus of corporate innovation is best angled towards persistent growth through tapping into the genius inside our organisation. It's not the role of a few people inside an organisation, but *all* people inside an organisation.

Innovation is hard. And time consuming. A discipline that needs to be mastered, managed and continuously improved upon. Innovation needs to be about less time spent on strategy or building kudos around the executive table, and more about time doing the hard work of conceptual development.

A NEW APPROACH TO INNOVATION

We need to think of innovation as a two-speed model inside the organisation. Your strategy and the program of work, plus your everyday operations, is the steady state, consistent approach of the first speed in your business. In simplistic terms, this is everything you plan to do to keep the lights on and move towards your strategic growth targets. There's a distinctive role for innovation in this process through understanding the known gaps you may have in your strategy, products, services or any other areas of your organisation. Dedicating time and resources to support the development of solutions for these gaps, whether they are innovative or not, will be required to achieve the identified short-, medium- and long-term goals of the organisation.

The top-down approach

The thinking required in the first speed of innovation in the organisation is a well-trodden path and one that many strategy teams spend a considerable amount of time thinking, planning and budgeting for. This top-down directive approach to innovation is driven by the ambition and vision of the company. The unspoken problem with a top-down approach is that the majority of the organisation sees this as someone else's job.

When misaligned innovation programs and values are spruiked by leaders of an organisation, they fall flat when only a small, select group in the organisation feels part of the process. I know this is not the typical company line, and is something that executives and leaders don't want to hear. The truth stings. But only focusing on innovation through this channel becomes exclusionary and prohibits this from being a real and meaningful part of the culture.

Innovation through a top-down process is important, and will always have a role to play in a broader and more inclusive innovation ecosystem. We need the focus of these incredible minds to look up and outside the organisation to build a vision and growth trajectory for the organisation.

The bottom-up approach

The second speed is made up of the ad-hoc, opportunistic and unplanned innovation ideas. These are the unknowns. The ideas we didn't see coming. Often the ones we have no idea what to do with.

These are the ideas that haven't been generated in the strategy and innovation teams, and in some cases they are not linked to strategy at all. They are coming directly from a person who deals with a consistent problem or is customer-facing and has thought of a new way of doing something or giving the customer what they really want.

It is this second speed of innovation that's often overlooked, or the people in the organisation are unsure what to do with it, or they feel they simply have no place in the process. The ideas, genius, talent and wisdom of these employees can go to waste if they are not provided the opportunities, space and process to work through their ideas. Looking down and in to the organisation through this process is equally as important.

In a two-speed model, the ideas in the second speed will ebb and flow, and they will not be consistent. These innovation ideas come from your employees, and often from the unlikeliest of places. Without ideas there will be no innovation. This is not saying that every idea that comes from your employees is relevant, worthy of investment and able to create value. Of course, that will not be the case. But the value goes beyond the ideas and the bottom line value they may bring. It's in the development and growth of a culture of innovation and high performance that will provide the tangible and intangible benefits.

This bottom-up approach to innovation is where the culture of innovation is nourished and cultivated to create an inclusive approach that will over time lift the skills and output of the entire organisation.

THE INNOVATION ECOSYSTEM

Innovation needs to be a systematic, integrated ecosystem that everyone in the organisation participates in, and not a separate and secret black box for a select few individuals. An optimal innovation ecosystem is one where the top-down and bottom-up processes meet in the middle in a functional innovation portfolio, with a mandate to optimise, prioritise and deliver cross-functional, collaborative benefits for the long-term growth of the organisation. This is not some type of innovation utopia, or an elusive unicorn approach. This is an achievable outcome when a dedicated framework and process, as well as tools and resources are in place. I will show you the steps to put a robust framework in place to create an innovation ecosystem that will add value, create a culture of innovation, and find the inner genius inside your organisation.

Innovation is a desirable, aspirational and achievable outcome for any organisation; you just need to take a step back to develop an ecosystem that's going to have long-term outcomes that add value. Think of your current innovation program or aspirations like a caterpillar turning into a butterfly. They don't just slap on wings and become the beautiful creatures we see in the world and they are good to go. It's an evolutionary process that requires change in the form of metamorphosis, and there is no going back. Caterpillars have to dissolve into a pile of goo to become butterflies.

I don't want your innovation program to dissolve into a pile of goo; I do want you to understand that it will require a metamorphosis of sorts. To truly have an embedded innovation ecosystem that's more than just words on a page, an organisation needs to rethink their approach to innovation and rebuild a process that makes it part of its lifeblood.

IT WILL NOT BE EASY

The framework I teach my clients is simple in theory, but the challenges and nuances are always in the implementation. Think of it like your own organisational metamorphosis process. It'll take a considerable amount of time, effort, energy, and a lot of dedicated focus to get there. It will not be easy. It will be full of setbacks. I am not going to pretend that it's going to be a walk in the park and the more you hustle the better you'll be. This is not a ra-ra entrepreneurial puff piece full of motivational speeches and mic-dropping moments. Rather, the purpose of this book is to provide you with a functional, step-by-step framework to embed innovation inside your organisation and make it part of the pulse of your business.

We're going to confront head-on the dark side of innovation and the reasons why innovation fails in a corporate setting. It's time to debunk some myths and rewire our thinking to look past the perceived sexiness of innovation and focus on the hard work and tenacity required to create a functional innovation portfolio. Would you still do it if we took 'innovation' out of your title?

If it were easy, more than just 1.9% of organisations would have a fully integrated, repeatable, scalable and pervasive innovation eco-system in their organisation. Like all changes and new programs, this will not be an overnight success for your organisation. It will take time, patience and dedicated focus from people at all levels. An integrated innovation ecosystem is something that needs to be nurtured and developed throughout its entire lifecycle.

I'm going to give you the framework to rethink and re-establish innovation inside your organisation to remove the theatre of inno-vation and help you embed a functional, holistic ecosystem that encompasses the entire organisation and adds value to the bottom line.

The 10 keys to a successful innovation program

If you don't listen to the ideas of your employees,
you will eventually be left with an organisation of
people with nothing to say ...

What does it really look like to have an innovation ecosystem inside your organisation? It's about the interaction and interconnectedness of innovation throughout the entire organisation, which has the capacity to utilise and include all areas and people within the organisation. It's not having a separate section detached and removed from the rest of the organisation. Does this sound like your organisation? If not, it's time to rethink how you are setting your innovation program up for success.

To build a successful innovation ecosystem there are 10 key things you need to do:

1. Remove the theatre of innovation.

2. Cultivate a culture of pervasive curiosity to encourage the development of ideas.

3. Leverage internal creativity and genius.

4. Make your process repeatable, scalable and pervasive – innovation is a doing word.

5. Understand that innovation isn't an extracurricular activity.

6. Make innovation a core part of your business rhythm.

7. Balance innovation and risk.

8. Democratise innovation – it isn't about the technology, product or 'the one thing'.

9. Allow innovation leaders to drive your culture.

10. Celebrate your successes, achievements, wins and losses.

Innovation is more than a product, service or visionary dream. Innovation is a community attitude inside your organisation, which is passionate, persistent, collaborative, knowledge-seeking and inclusive. It's not the idea of one person, or the work of one small team. It's an attitude that brings together diverse ideas, differing opinions, a multi-disciplinary approach to enablement, and a desire to elevate the skills and knowledge of everyone in the community. Friction and competing priorities are inevitable, and they are managed through a process of mutual respect.

Wow! That's a bit of an Innovation Manifesto. Sound like your organisation? If it doesn't, what are you missing?

An innovation ecosystem inside an organisation is so much more than a set of processes. The focus needs to be on humanising the process, giving your people a vision of where you are all going together, providing a suitable budget, and having a clear and easy process to follow.

If you truly want a culture of innovation, give it the respect it deserves.

Corporate Innervation Operating Systems that add real value to the bottom line focus on two key areas:

- Firstly, you need a framework, and this I am giving you in the latter part of this book.

- Secondly, you need to focus on the vision, people and culture.

You will never have a complete solution unless you do both.

The 10 steps to establishing a corporate innervation ecosystem will require you to rethink the process you have in place today and really consider what will genuinely add value. Go through these 10 key requirements and consider what you need to do to ensure your innovation ecosystem will be successful.

REMOVE THE THEATRE OF INNOVATION

Hackathons, pitch-fests, labs, competitions and any of the other hyped-up, ra-ra processes are all fun, high-visibility initiatives – but they don't deliver results. This is often the first step a leader goes to when they're looking to create a culture of innovation. Are they looking for staff engagement, or are they seeking a funnel of ideas? If leaders are just looking for some ideas there is an easier way to gather ideas to work through.

Innovation theatre treats ideas as though they are execution challenges and overlooks the obvious – that these ideas are full of unknowns and need to be worked through. Rarely are deployable results achieved through these mechanisms because they produce high-level ideas, and a pitch constructed in a vacuum doesn't articulate the work required to go from fun and imaginative idea to value-driving, deployable innovation.

This is not to say that every idea that comes out of innovation theatre needs to be dismissed. Absolutely not. I have no doubt some cracking ideas come out of this process from time to time. The problem is that ideas are cheap, easy and fast. Ideas, technology and innovation theatre are often the crutch of leaders and organisations seeking to 'look' innovative.

This may seem like a harsh judgement, but a distinction needs to be made between the theatre of innovation and the delivery of real, deployable innovation ideas. What happens when the show is over and the beanbags have been put away?

The real question you need to be asking is how do you manage, assess and build out these ideas? Do you have a process and supporting framework to manage this? Or do you send the winning team off to do the work as an extracurricular activity?

If there is a commitment of time, resources and money to turn these ideas into business models and deployable innovations then you are moving beyond the theatre of innovation. If nothing happens after such events or no value is created, why do they even exist in your organisation?

The participants in the theatre can end up feeling a bit jaded and short-changed because they participated through their time, energy and ideas, and inevitably they want to see some action taken. If you want to rapidly disengage your employees from an innovation program or presenting ideas, do nothing with them.

CULTIVATE A CULTURE OF PERVASIVE CURIOSITY

If you're not continually looking, questioning and opening your mind to new ways of doing things you'll miss new ideas. And the same goes for your employees. If they are not encouraged to flex their curiosity muscle and constructively question what's happening around them, there's an excellent chance they'll squash any ideas they have. We're so busy in our day-to-day roles, filled with deadlines and pressures, that we allow our curiosity muscle to waste away because we think we don't have time for it.

We forget that learning is a measurable outcome. We need to consider thinking as a creative process to solve our business problems, and you can measure this. As the culture of innovation grows and more employees become involved with the framework, you can start to see the demonstration of knowledge, processes, skills and values on both innovation and non-innovation projects.

Work to develop a culture of pervasive curiosity that is a conscious 24/7 approach, rather than something that's switched on and off. As an organisation we want to be continually learning, growing and fostering a level of curiosity to solve problems and seek better solutions from all employees. Encourage employees to ask questions that challenge current thinking and help move you away from doing things the way you have always done them, just because you always did it that way. This isn't change for the sake of it. It's questions evoked through a desire to look at everything through a lens of curiosity for the betterment of the organisation.

Curiosity cannot be mistaken for creativity. The two do have a symbiotic relationship, but for innovation to work you really need to be curious about a problem or situation to think creatively about it. To look at something from a different angle, a different perspective. Curiosity requires asking questions, learning something new, challenging the status quo, and not assuming we know all the answers.

Think of curiosity like a muscle. You need to work out constantly to maintain any gains. Don't force employees to innovate on demand and come up with lists of random ideas. Encourage them to continually question the world around them. Each person's perspective is their reality and how they view their world. Spending time asking questions can help encourage an empathetic view to see things from a different perspective. Many of the great innovations occurred through curiosity, an empathetic process and incremental failures. If we don't think to ask the questions, how will we know what we're missing?

An empathetic mindset will be required so your employees can learn more by doing, putting themselves in the users' shoes. Jump, boots and all, into the process of learning and evolving to get better. Curiosity, creation and innovation are lifelong journeys of learning. There will never be a point where we've 'got it' and have it mastered. It's important to understand that the more we see, the less we know, and it's this 'beginner's mind' that needs to be encouraged in our employees to support a lifelong journey of curiosity and learning.

Learning through failure and accepting this is part of the process. Failure is a dirty word in the corporate landscape, and while there is a lot of talk about failing fast and failing forward, it's still not something organisations are comfortable with. Finding out an idea is not going to work after you have taken it through a structured process isn't a failure, and it's important to acknowledge that this is part of the process. These valuable learnings need to be supported and encouraged.

Failure is something we fear, and we need to recognise this. Fear changes our mindset and can stop us from doing anything. We can get paralysis by analysis if we hold on to the fear of failure. Curiosity and the pursuit of a solution to a problem can be a great antidote to this fear of failure. We need to embrace the fear and get comfortable being uncomfortable.

LEVERAGE INTERNAL CREATIVITY AND GENIUS

Cultivate the knowledge, wisdom and collective experiences of the people in your organisation to build a knowledge bank. Understand that the people who know and best understand your organisation, customers and all the problems are the people who work in the organisation. Your people have the ideas and inspiration. They have been ruminating and conceptualising scenarios in their heads since they started. Your people are a core asset in your Corporate Innervation Operating System.

So often organisations and leaders look to outside experts for ideas or want to replicate an idea they have seen in another organisation or competitor. It can be a wise move to meet the market and ensure market share isn't eroded to competitors, but this shouldn't be the only source of information to guide innovation ideas.

If you don't listen to the ideas of your employees, you will eventually be left with an organisation of people with nothing to say. Read that last sentence again and let it really sink in. The organisations and leaders that really get this understand how to humanise the process to capture their internal genius. Your people are your competitive advantage for innovation.

Generating ideas, actioning them and being part of an innovation process is contagious. Listening to your employees and engaging them in the process supports the development of a culture of respect, high performance and continuous growth.

MAKE YOUR PROCESS REPEATABLE, SCALABLE, AND PERVASIVE

On its own, an idea has no value. Ideas without action are useless. Innovation occurs in the actions we take and not in the idea itself. Without a framework, process, methodology to prototype and test, and a portfolio to manage it all, you are just fluffing around with ideas. Sometimes they are actioned, but mostly they are not.

You must make it easy for ideas to be assessed and, when appropriate, tested. You need a clear, simple and structured end-to-end process from idea to implementation that's standardised across your organisation to ensure a repeatable and scalable process for innovation. Getting this right is the first step to innovation becoming pervasive in your organisation.

When you focus on the results only, you slow down progress. When you focus on your system, you are able to amplify your results by iteratively working through a defined process.

The flipside of this is when organisations confuse the systems with real innovation. All too often organisations focus on 'Agile', design thinking or other methodologies and think that this alone makes them innovative. Or they rely on these methodologies to draw out the innovations as they go. I don't want to mandate the type of delivery methodology you use in your organisation, but I do want you to understand that it will not bring innovation to your organisation.

'Agile' is one of the many project delivery methodologies that seems to be infiltrating businesses everywhere, and there is now even an Agile process for family meetings to help manage the chaos, get along better and reduce stress. Hmm … okay. It seems we are really trying to put a square peg in a round hole. Agile is an incredible method to build collaborative processes and for organising teams to support a working solution that's responsive and able to be nimble and flexible if changes are required. It's also fabulous at providing transparency on the deliverables, dependencies, blockages and how the team are relying on each other for delivery.

As a methodology for development and delivery, I love Agile. I am a huge advocate. But it will not make you an innovator, just like it won't make the emotive relationships of family any less chaotic. We need to understand the place and role of these methodologies as tools to support the process of delivery. These tools will help make your process repeatable and pervasive in your business. You need to think of them like an engine. If you put the wrong type of fuel in, or not enough fuel, its not going to get you where you want to go.

Create a practice of innovation inside your organisation that supports the development, delivery and process of taking ideas from their embryonic stage to deployment. The key to doing innovation right is understanding the tools and delivery methodologies you use inside the organisation are only one of the many aspects of the Corporate Innervation Operating System.

You will need to forge an innovation way of working inside your organisation that will deliver value, be easy and accessible for everyone to use, and focus on the overarching commitment to the delivery of innovation. Don't get caught in the trap of being defined by one particular methodology or set of rituals. In step five of the framework I look at how to create a process that is scalable, repeatable and pervasive for innovation in your organisation.

UNDERSTAND THAT INNOVATION ISN'T AN EXTRACURRICULAR ACTIVITY

Innovation isn't a side project that you do when you have nothing else to do! So don't ask your employees to fit it in during their spare time. Make it an essential portfolio that has the same weight and priority as your core business. If you want an effective innovation program that delivers genuine value, you must make adequate staff and resources available.

And while you're at it, don't skimp on the acknowledgement of your employees. If your employees are working hard on an innovation to develop an idea, make sure this is reflected in their key performance indicators, annual performance review, or whatever mechanism is used to evaluate performance. Make this a fluid process for employees and encourage metrics or a scorecard for those who participate, to accommodate this new and additional work.

If this is different to their substantive role, which it generally is, it's like they are provided only a nominal metric in their review. This is discouraging and sends the wrong message to employees. If we value innovation, we have to value the people who are working to develop innovative ideas.

It's more than the posters on the wall and the words in the values and vision statement. If you want it to be more than aspiration, it must be a core part of the organisation. Your employees will not take it seriously if the organisation doesn't. Create an innovation portfolio and program of work with a level of importance and priority that is understood by the people who will implement it.

MAKE INNOVATION A CORE PART OF YOUR BUSINESS RHYTHM

Innovation is not a competition between business units – it's a collaborative process. Don't let innovation be squirreled away to secret side projects and processes that are separate from the rest of the organisation. Make your innovation program part of the communication, processes and interactions that happen between all areas of the organisation every day to create the flow and collaboration process.

The business rhythm is not a separate process, it is the flow of communication and work between teams and divisions to support seamless operations. Don't extract your innovation function and make it an exclusive process; you will inevitably stifle your innovation potential.

The key steps to developing an innovation business rhythm are:

- Document the strategic vision for innovation for inclusion in the annual strategic planning process, including support, resources and any other operations that may require collaboration from other divisions and teams.

- Create a guidance list of your requirements for the year ahead. Innovation will be difficult to plan for initially, and the first 12 to 24 months may be a process of testing the capability and capacity of the organisation. Over time, you'll be able to provide a more robust view based on the performance of previous years.

- Create a calendar of meetings you want to hold, including team meetings, leadership team and executive updates, schedule of meetings for innovation teams, and communications for the entire organisation.

- Work with Human Resources to develop a plan for utilising resources in collaborative teams and how that can be managed and documented correctly. Get this done early to remove any potential hiccups that may hold up the development of innovation teams.

- Document what is required to meet the deadlines and needs of the finance and risk teams. Know what is required of you, and by whom, and work this into your innovation rhythm. The fewer favours you need to call in, and the more you work with the processes the organisation has in place, the easier it will be to get innovation projects off the ground.

The goal here is for all key stakeholders to understand the requirements of the innovation function to support the development of a cadence for the innovation teams to deliver. This shouldn't be complex. Make it simple. You want this information to be used and understood by everyone to support the innovation portfolio.

The goal of innovation becoming a core part of your business rhythm is making sure all the key stakeholders and areas of the business know what to expect, and when, so a united focus can be established on delivering innovation projects.

BALANCE INNOVATION AND RISK

Innovation doesn't have to mean that you take outlandish risks. You don't need to – and shouldn't – bet the ranch on one idea. Risk is an essential part of any business, we just need to understand how much risk we're willing to take on in pursuit of an innovation strategy.

Just as the organisation as a whole defines its risk appetite to support the alignment of strategy and execution, this exercise also needs to occur for innovation.

To know how far you can take your innovation program, you must have an understanding of how much risk you are willing to take and how you plan to balance this with any opportunities that present themselves. The culture, flexibility and capability of the organisation needs to be considered in the determination of risk tolerances.

Your approach to risk needs to be about diversification and understanding the risk tolerances and capability of the organisation to deliver. Pursuing profitable innovations that may lead to a competitive advantage is more important than going down the path of an innovation the organisation or people are ill-equipped to deal with.

We need to be clear on the risk tolerances and boundaries the organisation is willing to work within. What's the point of developing a flashy product or service idea if you cannot deliver on the promise? Effective innovation is more important than flashy innovation.

Focus on creating and sustaining future value for the organisation and not on ideas and projects that may diminish value. It's not about cannibalising one area of the business to allow an idea to 'get up'. Corporate innovation should never be a zero-sum game. Ultimately you want the organisation to benefit as a whole from the innovation portfolio.

Be careful not to undermine innovation by not taking enough risks. It really is a balance that needs to be thought through and continually assessed. It's crucial the key stakeholders and leaders are open to healthy conflict and robust discussions to debate constructive ideas, to ensure they are taking the right level of risk and not holding onto out-of-date thinking and principles.

The slow, torturous and hard-to-watch death of the print media is an example of an industry that really bet the ranch on the wrong risk profile. An industry that was close to running a monopoly is now looking like a dinosaur about to become extinct. Why? Instead of seeing the evolution of digital media as an adjacency and transformation they needed to make, they continued to invest in costly newsprint systems, printing presses and manual circulation programs that simply cannot compete with digital publishing that doesn't have these overheads.

I'm not going to single out any particular organisation, as you can apply this story to almost all of the print newspapers across the globe. I am sure you can name a print newspaper that tried to jam their print business model into a website. And then they tried to apply the old business model of paid subscriptions. The days of a newspaper having a monopoly in their region are long gone – the digital environment means there is an abundance of free news, sports, weather, opinions and everything else readers are used to seeing in their print news-paper, online and for free. They played the wrong hand, and were too slow to understand they lost their monopoly status.

Plummeting profits have left many print newspapers struggling to be able to respond effectively and to remain relevant. Of course, there are some smart and savvy news agencies that developed online subscription models with carefully curated content that their readers are willing to pay for, but there are only a few of these.

This shows what can happen when you don't balance the risks of innovation correctly. A digital environment didn't change how many people wanted to read the news, it changed how they wanted to read it, and the industry was too busy trying to defend an old way of doing things and their customers left them behind.

DEMOCRATISE INNOVATION - IT ISN'T ABOUT THE TECHNOLOGY, PRODUCT OR 'THE ONE THING'

It will not be the ideas or that 'one thing' that make your organisation innovative. Ideas are cheap, easy, and they can happen really fast. It really isn't difficult to develop a large funnel of new and exciting innovation ideas. It's also easy to pick off some low-hanging fruit, have some really quick wins, and think you have established long-term successful change.

A truly successful corporate innovation process requires you to change the way you think, feel, manage, report and organise innovation.

You can wear the T-shirts and sit on beanbags, but to be effective you will need to create a shift in the hearts and minds of the people in the organisation. It's about leading by doing and making innovation available to everyone. This is about democratising innovation to make it a process and way of working that's accessible and available to everyone.

This is integral for building new revenue streams, while at the same time creating new levels of engagement and social capital inside the organisation. This isn't about making innovation an unmonitored process where everyone innovates on their own thing at their own pace. Rather, it's about creating access and involving employees in the creative process, thereby increasing their sense of ownership over the process and the speed of delivery.

Corporate Innervation is about the people inside your organisation, and it's critical that the process is humanised to make it an inclusive process. Creating an inclusive process will support the development of knowledge for all people inside the organisation. This will result in a more efficient process because your employees are no longer waiting for their leaders to tell them what to do next; they are building the strategy and program of work from the bottom up.

ALLOW INNOVATION LEADERS TO DRIVE YOUR CULTURE

Select innovation leaders who understand it's not their job to be 'innovation gurus' or the oracle of all new ideas, rather their role is to coach, guide and mentor innovation. The innovation itself and the cross-functional collaborative team that has been put together to incubate an idea are the heroes. Innovation cultures are created through the people and how the processes and protocols are consistently used by the people.

While this isn't a book about leadership per se, it needs to be clear that if you have the wrong innovation leaders in place it will have negative implications for the future of innovation in your organisation. Your innovation culture is created, sustained and transformed by the people you entrust it to. You've created a vision, values, strategy and processes to develop innovation inside your organisation, so don't tie yourself down before you've started the race by putting the wrong people in the leadership positions.

The leaders you entrust with your innovation culture set the tone for what will happen on a day-to-day basis for innovation, and ultimately whether you will successfully build a positively evolving innovation culture. While it's important you have people who understand the rules of the game and who coach and guide from a place of experience and wisdom, they are not the most important elements. Attitude and an inclusive leadership approach based on humility and not hubris are the characteristics you need to hire or appoint on. Appoint the person on what they can do, and the way you believe they can embed change and culture. You can't teach attitude, but you can teach the tools, processes and framework to make it work.

Culture is invisible. It is not something you can see or touch, but when it's working, it's like you are operating a well-oiled machine where people trust each other, and the magic happens. Culture usually isn't as strong as we want it to be, and it only takes one fox in the henhouse to create significant setbacks or destroy the culture you have been working hard to establish.

Your innovation leaders are there to manage and develop a portfolio of innovation ideas through a process of continuous learning, development and support. These are the people you need to make it happen. They need to understand their role, and know that it isn't about them but about how they support the growth and development of the people to allow innovation to occur. When you have leaders like this, you have the right people to help you embed innovation in your organisation.

CELEBRATE YOUR SUCCESSES, ACHIEVEMENTS, WINS AND LOSSES

Innovation isn't a sure thing. The only thing that is guaranteed is the process. You really need to fall in love with the grind, because there is no crystal ball to predict how each project will turn out. Of course, you can follow all the steps in your framework, work with your customers, research and model all the various scenarios based on every variable you can think of, but all that will provide you with is an excellent estimation for what may occur. The events of 2020 show us that no matter how well planned out or prepared you may be, unplanned externalities may destroy your best plans.

Not every idea will be successful. If you are going to develop an innovation portfolio, it needs to be full of ideas that are focused on the growth, customer satisfaction and future revenue streams of the organisation, not just ideas you think are guaranteed to be successful. If you already know the outcome, is it really innovation? Or just a tick-the-box exercise?

You know you have an evolving corporate innovation culture when you are focused on the development of ideas that make sense for the organisation, you don't care whether they are the sexy ideas, and you are centred on the process and development of information for future growth.

We can often learn more from a failure than we can from the best success. Failures that have occurred through a rigorous process, considered thinking, and testing a number of possible hypotheses are never bad. But what I often see organisations do is try to brush aside these outcomes so they can shine the light on the successful projects.

We need to acknowledge the work, effort and time put into an idea – regardless of the outcome. Showcasing what you did, the research, hypotheses tested and all the steps you took in a failed innovation project needs to be seen as a great learning and development tool. Also, you never know how that information may be used elsewhere in the organisation, or for another idea.

Who would've thought that a product as unsexy as foam latex would lead a revolution in the make-up and special effects world, as it's an unsophisticated product and certainly not among the high-tech solutions we expect from the movie industry. John Chambers, Rick Baker and Dick Smith – not together but on separate projects and movies – worked to develop products and methodologies to create special effects make-up for movies that looked real and reduced the reliance on computer-generated graphics, which in the 1980s could be extremely cost prohibitive.

Individually and together they shared their knowledge, experiments, failures and successes to establish a formula and process to create the monsters we know and love in movies today, everything from *An American Werewolf in London*, *Planet of the Apes*, and *Star Wars* to the dinosaurs of *Jurassic Park*. These same formulas and techniques are still used in the movies you watch today, like the current release (as I write this) *The Invisible Man*.

What is so incredible about this story is these people were all focused on using their innovative techniques, new formulas and processes to build and grow the market, so they generously shared their knowledge and instructions with anyone who wanted to learn. Famously, if a special effects artist wrote to Dick Smith seeking information about a particular technique, he wrote back with instructions, recommendations for materials, and a step-by-step guide. And he personally typed it out. What a legend!

Through the nature of their sharing of both failures and successes, these giants in the special effects industry built their own ecosystem of innovation to elevate the business of movie special effects make-up. Even though they were competitors, they understood that a collaborative approach would elevate their whole industry, and this benefits not just them, but future generations of special effects make-up artists.

* * *

Corporate Innervation is about building an innovation ecosystem based around the humans inside your organisation. Your ecosystem will not be sustained by the systems and tools that you implement, rather it will grow and develop through a community that is passionate, persistent and collaborative.

Reflect on the innovation process in your organisation and interconnectedness of what you are trying to achieve throughout the organisation. If you don't have an aligned, human-based process you can start small and work through these steps:

1. Focus on building a real innovation portfolio to add value and remove the theatre of innovation.

2. Innovation can occur through making small things better every day, so work to cultivate a culture of pervasive curiosity to encourage the development of ideas.

3. Put your people at the heart of your innovation program to leverage internal creativity and genius.

4. Innovation requires dedicated effort, practice, and support, so give your people a process that is repeatable, scalable, and pervasive so it can become part of your way of working.

5. Give innovation the respect it deserves and make it a core program of work, not an extracurricular activity.

6. Innovation isn't a side project – make it a core part of your business rhythm.

7. Understand what considered risks you are willing to take to balance innovation and risk for future growth.

8. Build social capital inside your organisation by democratising innovation and allowing your people to tell you what your internal and external customers need.

9. Find leaders who work to grow, enhance and support everyone to develop, to drive your innovation culture.

10. Create a culture of knowledge sharing through celebrating all aspects of innovation and learning, including the successes and failures.

You're not a startup, so stop behaving like one

True innovation lies in making small things better for the customer every day.

Innovation is really having its moment in the spotlight. Everyone is talking about it. We see it as the shining light for future growth and transformation. But few corporates are doing it well.

Innovation has unfortunately turned into a bit of a hype and ra-ra process, where it's looked to for both motivation and hero worshipping. Innovation has the image as the cool, popular kid inside the organisation that everyone wants to hang around with. On social media, in the press, and the way we discuss our corporate values make innovation look sexy, a little mysterious and aspirational. It's so easy to get swept up in this because the media and information we see is skewed towards the incredible success stories, with particular attention on the unicorn businesses.

My experience with executive leadership teams is they want to be part of the hype and hustle and 'act like a startup'. They want to move fast, be disruptive and focus on digital transformation. But let's be honest – digital transformation in the corporate space is not something we can define as innovation and experimental. This is a strategic initiative, one that will be burdened with process, metrics, bureaucracy, and the overarching culture of the company.

The challenge with acting like a startup is that it generally doesn't align with the way larger organisations operate. As a generalisation, a startup doesn't have a structured way of working because they are often small and independent, are frequently pivoting as they move through a process of test and measure, and accept that profit, if any, will be delayed. While a startup often has a mission and is value driven, who and what they are is often defined along the journey.

Larger organisations have defined value propositions, brand equity in the market and an established culture. It needs to be recognised that whatever the culture is, and whether it's good or bad, it's the one the organisation has today and it is likely to be ingrained. An organisation's culture and market perceptions rarely change quickly.

When organisations and leaders are seduced into the hustle culture of behaving like a startup, it's often because they want to operate in this market but under the safety net of being paid. It's really, really tough out there in the startup market, where over 90% fail. That's some tough odds. It's no wonder so many people seek to live out their entrepreneurial dreams inside the shelter of an organisation.

A good idea doesn't guarantee success in the market. What is so easily forgotten are the masses of failed ideas that never even made it to market, the amount of dollars lost chasing a dream idea, or even the number of iterations or failed attempts it took to get something right.

We need to learn a new way of looking at innovation and what that means in the context of an organisation. Time to dust off the glitter and gloss and see innovation for what it really is and how it really works. Change your mindset and focus away from the cool and fun ideas, and lean in to the development of a portfolio of ideas that will enhance everything you do and set your organisation up for long-term sustainable growth.

WHY DO WE FOCUS SO MUCH ON DISRUPTION, AND NOT ON THE IDEAS THAT WILL ADD VALUE TO OUR BOTTOM LINE?

Innovation teams seem to be everywhere, and in every organisation. Designathons, innovation labs, hackathons, a-ha moments, beanbag rooms, ping-pong tables, bootcamps, pitchfests – the list of innovation theatre goes on and on and on. The theatre of innovation draws leadership teams in because they can perform the role of innovation without having to deliver any tangible results. These are things you do when you want to *look* innovative but don't really want to 'do' any innovation.

I get it. This is done partly because it's fun, engaging, and a break from the norm of our day-to-day jobs. Your employees feel seen and heard in the moment. That moment crashes really quickly when the lights go off and everyone returns to their day jobs and the pitch, idea, or design slowly fades into the background. Forgotten. Backlogged. Or it just never quite gets any resources or money in the budget process. These innovation theatre activities can be really fun, but they very rarely deliver a deployable innovation idea that adds value to the bottom line.

It's too easy to be distracted by bright, shiny ideas that seem fun and different. Who doesn't want to bring the 'next big idea' to market? These ideas can be distracting, and often take people's focus away from their true objective. I spend a lot of time working with innovation leaders and executive teams, coaching them to build an internal innovation discipline. Innovation isn't something that happens by chance or luck. It's a skill honed through a process-driven multi-disciplinary approach to evidence-based insights, customer-centric design, iterative development, and business thinking that bridges the gap between the current strategy and where we want to go tomorrow.

We're looking to be different, futuristic, creative, and it all sounds like a huge amount of fun and it's exciting to be on the bleeding edge of the future direction of the organisation. But the hype from all this needs to be removed, along with the mindset that one idea, one working group or the theatre of innovation will tick the box and make the organisation 'innovative'.

True innovation lies in making small things better for the customer every day. Disruption can only occur when customers are dissatisfied, or you are not giving them what they want or need. Don't create the hole in the market for someone else to fill.

Disruptions often occur when new businesses enter the market because they either fill a gap or remove activities that are not being delivered well for customers. They generally don't have better technology or a more innovative way of doing something. They're just doing the things that make the customer happy. Customers tend to not leave when they are satisfied. But if they can have a better experience, of course they'll leave.

Disruption starts with unhappy customers

If you are being disrupted, it's because your customers are driving the process. So, if disruption starts with unhappy customers, shouldn't the focus be on your customers and everything you need to do to improve their experience? If you are not listening to your customers they will go elsewhere. This all sounds like common sense, and for many people I know I will be preaching to the converted, but why then do we focus our innovation programs on trying to be like start-ups and disrupters?

Netflix are often touted as disrupters, and to some extent they were when they initially entered the market. In the early days when they entered the market in 1997 to compete directly with Blockbuster and other movie rental chains, they struggled. Renting DVDs via mail was tough, and certainly not the instantaneous experience we know and love today. So, when video streaming became more accessible and cost effective, in 2007 Netflix were able to pivot quickly to offer this service.

More than ever they focused on the customer experience to understand how to make it as seamless, efficient and enjoyable as possible. Now they are disrupting both the free-to-air and the pay TV market.

To give customers what they want they pioneered the use of artificial intelligence and machine learning in this space to create a consumer experience that is tailored to viewing tastes. Netflix is just one of many in this marketplace now, with new ideas and services looking to disrupt them every day. Now Netflix is the big corporate behemoth, and instead of looking to disrupt the market and behave like a startup, they are doubling down on what they do best: making sure they provide what the customer wants in a way they love.

Netflix's core strength lies in their ability to understand what their customers want using a combination of in-depth analytics and behavioural data. Focusing on every element of their customer experience in order to grow with their customers' changing needs means they are in effect continuing to lead the market, while protecting themselves from potential disruption. They are not implementing traditional protectionist strategies of price, acquisition or crowding out, because there is an understanding that growing the market for all creates more opportunity overall.

Today they are more than just a streaming service, they are curators of content, a film studio and a production house. Netflix's advancement into the film development and production market was done not to disrupt the market but to create a film and distribution model that suited the evolving needs of their customers. They know intimately what their customers want, and are focused on building for the customer, which is driving their success.

In 2019, Netflix made more movies than any other film studio, releasing over 60 films, even having some films nominated for Oscars. Who would've thought a content streamer would become bigger than the institution of Hollywood? This wasn't a battle of cinema against streaming services, as there is a place in the market for both at this stage. This wasn't about blowing up the market, rather it was about non-disruptive creation of an abundant market that not only provides more content for customers, but drives a broader market for the writers, film and television makers, directors, and a whole industry of people involved in the production of content.

I know I'm stating the obvious when I say as an organisation you need to focus on your core strengths, the things that make you distinctive, and then double down on them. When you get this right and understand the needs of your customer, you can not only defend against disruption, but you'll have the capabilities to outlast market challenges and give yourself the time to build great innovations.

FALL IN LOVE WITH THE PROCESS OF INNOVATION TO REINVENT YOUR UNDERSTANDING OF INNOVATION IN YOUR ORGANISATION

Organisations run on processes. Whether we like it or not, the reason organisations grow and continue to operate is because they have repeatable, scalable and pervasive processes and systems for consistent execution. This is done to reduce risk, and – in some instances – it does reduce the organisation's ability to be agile and lean.

Innovation is a disciplined process. It can't be a free-for-all, anything-goes approach to the development of innovation ideas, and they can't be shipped off to a lab to be developed in isolation in the hopes of being 'agile'. It's time for your organisation to fall in love with the rituals, process and endless knowledge-seeking required to deliver a great innovation idea, rather than just the outcome itself. Ideas are cheap and easy. Ideas on their own are completely useless. There's no hero coming to rescue any of these ideas and turn them into a fully functional, deployable, revenue-earning success.

There's really nothing mysterious about the process of innovation ecosystems inside a corporate environment. For innovation to be successful, a balance needs to be found between process, mindset and multi-disciplinary techniques required to bring a deployable innovation to market. The mystery lies in the customer, the people, and managing the process through a culture.

The key to a great innovation culture that has longevity and success in the organisation is implementation of a Corporate Innervation Operating System – which I have outlined for you in this book – that focuses on building a portfolio of ideas for growth, development, and solving the internal and external customer gaps, challenges and problems.

As someone who has worked with many clients, my own startups, and individuals to bring successful innovations and ecosystems to life, often in crowded markets, I can tell you that it isn't a sexy process. There are sleepless nights, continuous research, endless pivots, reframing of business models, ideas that just don't work, and coffee … lots and lots of coffee. It's about falling in love with your customer, understanding them to solve their needs, and working out the best way to do this.

It sounds easy, but like everything, implementation is hard.

I personally love it because I thrive on being continuously challenged, seeking solutions, and solving problems that other people have overlooked. And on understanding the customer mindset in order to deliver something that makes sense, rather than something that is driven by ego or the technical wow factor.

Fall in love with the smart, focused and customer-focused innovation solutions that will not only support the continued growth of your organisation, but will develop and elevate the skills of your people.

FORGET ABOUT THE 'DISRUPTION' PROJECTS

Aiming to be the disrupter of the market and conquer all of your competitors is a little myopic and quite frankly not smart. Innovation done only to make a short-term impact will often only be a distraction, and may lead to a portfolio of expensive, ineffective projects. A less disruptive innovation can often provide better and more long-term results. If you want your innovation program to be sustainable, you need to be able to implement, manage and own the space appropriately.

Let's face it, there's often a ton of ego involved in innovation. A lot of people get involved for the thrill of the possible disruption, the creation of a unicorn, and because they want to be a 'startup' with the safety net of a full-time wage. I see a lot of this in the corporate world, but this isn't the opportunity to live out your entrepreneurial dream if it doesn't support the long-term vision of the organisation. And it most likely won't.

Ideas that people simply like are distractions that need to be avoided. For this to work, everyone who participates in corporate innovation needs to leave their ego at the door because it will not be needed for any part of the process. Open minds and humility will be required for every step of the process. The most effective innovation programs, and the ones with longevity, are those that focus on filling the gaps for future growth. As a result, they are often the less edgy and less sexy ones, but you don't want to bet the ranch on something because it's a bit edgy … it's wise strategy to hedge your bets and put your customer at the heart of your thinking.

CREATE A POWERFUL VISION OF YOUR CUSTOMER TODAY AND TOMORROW

The purpose isn't just to be innovative because it's fun. Nor is it solely about providing a value-add program for your employees. The purpose should be to develop an ecosystem for innovation that becomes self-perpetuating and sustains itself through the revenue it generates. This isn't hard in theory, but it does require time, diligence and dedicated focus on the development of the process internally. The Corporate Innervation Operating System will guide you through the steps to develop and implement a framework that works.

A key element of this is removing the ideas and theatre of innovation that are purely distractions. Create a powerful vision of your customer today and tomorrow so your innovation portfolio is dedicated to the creation of meeting their future needs and growing the market. Reframe your thinking of disruption and companies like Netflix. Instead of putting them on a pedestal for disruption, understand how they use their in-depth knowledge of their customer to focus their innovation, which is what stops them from being disrupted today.

Disruption can only occur when customers are dissatisfied. It's worth writing this on every wall and making it the catchcry for your innovation program. Make this the mantra of your team and everyone in the organisation. Instead of trying to be the disrupter, make your customers so happy and satisfied that they never want to leave.

Reframe the thinking towards the development of a portfolio of ideas that will have a positive impact on the customer, the organisation, and the overall market will be more powerful in the long run.

You won't get there with that one great idea. It's going to take time, dedication, consistent hard work, and hours and hours of effort to upskill and bring the knowledge of innovation to everyone in the organisation.

* * *

You know you've got all this right when you have a repeatable, scalable, and pervasive innovation process and culture in your organisation. Employees move on, and consultants to help you do this will come and go, all with their own ways of doing things and ideas on the world. Corporate innovation success will be determined by a framework, process and culture that's not dependent on your current leadership team or incumbent innovation manager or team. When your innovation ecosystem doesn't need you anymore because it's a dynamic, thriving process that is part of the DNA of the organisation, you know you have nailed it.

The good news is I'm giving you a step-by-step framework to follow to support the development of your corporate innovation ecosystem. Just don't skip straight there; like all elite performers you need to do the preparation and training before you step into the race.

How can you stop behaving like a startup?

1. Focus on your core strengths as an organisation to find the balance between process, mindset and multi-disciplinary techniques required to bring a deployable innovation to market.

2. Fall in love with the process of innovation – the hard work, endless research, testing and development – so you can remove the glitz and glamour that comes with success, because this is only 0.5% of what is seen.

3. Remove the focus on being disruptive in the market and turn attention on your customers to understand their needs, wants

and aspirations. Instead of being myopic in your view of innovation, broaden your thinking to create a position of growth to make your customers never want to leave.

4. Forget about trying to create the next one big thing, because you don't want to bet the ranch on one innovation. Create a diversified portfolio of ideas, because it takes time, dedication, and consistent hard work to upskill and bring the knowledge of innovation to the organisation.

5. Develop a powerful and deep understanding of your customer to enable you to move towards the development of an innovation ecosystem that becomes self-perpetuating and a long-term funnel of future ideas.

PART II

Dealing with the
demons of innovation

THERE'S A DARK SIDE to innovation that is rarely talked about. We don't like it, but we need to confront it head on. We don't want this to be us, but we've all been here and done these things. It's time to get comfortable being uncomfortable so we can debunk the myths, and get rid of the behaviours and mindsets that derail innovation in the corporate environment.

In this section I am going to dig into the real dark side of corporate innovation, and look at the reasons why it often fails and then becomes a money pit that adds no value. I'm not going to sugar coat it: this section is hard, icky, and talks about the issues I know leadership teams find uncomfortable. But innovation can't thrive without the right environment.

My passion is helping people find the extraordinary within their organisation and guiding the development of innovation teams, and to do this we sometimes need to look at the ugly side of the corporate world that we've all been a perpetrator of and on the receiving end of. None of us are innocent, including myself, but the only way to improve is to confront all of these issues and be brutally honest with ourselves, our teams and the culture we work within. We don't want this to be us, but we've all been there and done these things.

The purpose of this section isn't to demonise leaders, innovation teams or anyone else, rather it is designed to help you recognise the problems that cause corporate innovation programs to be lacklustre or fail.

Innovation cannot be done if we're all wearing rose-coloured glasses. You're not going to get to your desired state of innovation and growth if you've always done what you did in the past to get here today. Stay with me; I know this is going to be uncomfortable and a little confronting, but if we rip the Band-Aid off and have an honest look at what's underneath, then we can work to create a corporate innovation process that unlocks the genius inside your organisation.

The dark side of innovation

Innovation is not a zero-sum game, so leave your criticism, competitiveness and defensiveness at the door.

Innovation cultures of organisations are depicted as fun, dynamic and empowering places to work. We've all seen these values, attributes, and – I have to say – aspirations in the strategy and values documents of organisations. But unfortunately, their unexpectedly insidious nature, which is often a slow burn and not immediately obvious to those inside the organisation, erodes the future success of a corporate innovation framework.

We all want innovation to be fun and exciting, and we want to be the ones who come up with the world-class, game-changing idea that is 'the next big thing'. It is the desire for these outcomes, feelings and in some instances power that creates a real dark side to innovation. There's no point ignoring it or pretending it's not present in your organisation because I can guarantee you it is. Why? Human nature.

One thing I see a lot of is the inability to address the dark side and negative behaviours that innovation cultures can produce, which inevitably cause an innovation framework to fail. For something that seems to be so universally loved and desired, it often seems to be overlooked that innovation needs to be counterbalanced with some tougher behaviours and processes to ensure its success.

The dark side of innovation usually shows up through passive aggressive behaviour, no psychological safety to freely move through ideas and concepts, exclusion, and zero tolerance for failure. There are many others, but I am only going to address the most prevalent problems that erode the success of a corporate innovation framework.

Leaders without an open mind or confidence in their ability as a leader are often the biggest offenders in this space. It can be difficult to lead a team at the best of times, and innovation requires an understanding that outcomes are unknown and success is measured through dedication, commitment and continuous movement towards what can be only conceptual outcomes. (In chapter 8, I outline the skills and attributes your innovation leaders need to have to support a successful Corporate Innervation Operating System.)

CREATING PSYCHOLOGICAL SAFETY IN YOUR INNOVATION ECOSYSTEM

Let's start with the hardest and most toxic problem that occurs with the development and implementation of an innovation framework. To be fair, this is a problem that happens in other areas of organisations and their cultures, but I am only going to dig into this in the context of a corporate innovation ecosystem. This is the big, hairy, ugly issue of not having any psychological safety for people participating in and supporting the development and implementation of new ideas. Hands down, this is the number one driver of success or failure for a corporate innovation ecosystem. If you can get this right, and it's certainly not easy, it will support the positive management of these dark side problems.

Unfortunately, we probably all know someone in the workplace who feels clearly threatened by others' ideas. It can be disguised in many ways, from arrogance and disregard to fake sweetness that is just a mask disguising criticism, competitiveness and white-anting.

These behaviours can be very hard to pinpoint, making them difficult to manage and eradicate.

Psychological safety for your innovation ecosystem requires a combination of permission and access for all members to participate as equals, and respect for all ideas, participants and trust. When we can get to this point we know we can support the development of high-performing innovation teams because they know they will not be punished for mistakes. We need to allow people the space to stick their head up with a new concept or idea without the fear of having it cut off. Research shows the positive emotions that come with psychological safety – like trust, curiosity, confidence and inspiration – support the broadening of the mind to new ideas and ways of thinking.[1] It's in this state that we can open our mind to complex problems and we are better at divergent thinking, which is a core cognitive process to accessing our creative brain.

How to create a safe environment

Innovation requires motivation, resilience, persistence, and the ability to take risks. While this is a deep and complex subject, and I am only touching on it lightly here, I support the development of psychological safety with our innovation teams through the following:

1. **Criticism leads to a zero-sum game.** Criticism, competitiveness and disengagement from others' ideas is a trait of learned helplessness in the workforce, which is usually used to throw someone off balance and regain the position of power in the conversation. It's a classic corporate heavyweight move, particularly if someone feels there's an idea that they should have come up with and didn't, or an idea may result in unwanted changes in their division or team. Approach all conversations collaboratively with the knowledge that true success is a win–win situation.

---

1   University of North Carolina, Prof. Barbara Fredrickson.

Now, I'm not going to be Pollyanna about this and pretend that this works each and every time. It doesn't, and probably never will. There will always be a minority of people that only provide lip service to the values and will be two-faced. We've all seen it or been on the receiving end of it. But even in these situations, we need to approach any type of adversity with collaboration. It will be hard because logic and rational thinking will not always be the winner on the day, but it's important to be collaborative and avoid putting people offside, because as I discuss throughout this book, persistence and tenacity are key attributes of successful innovation teams. Play the long game in these situations and be willing to lose the battle to win the war.

2. **All voices are equal.** The removal of hierarchy and corporate or social status allows each member of the team to speak up and know their contribution will be valued, considered, appreciated, and have equal weighting. Instead of deferring to the most senior person on the team, we need to recognise the value each member of a collaborative team brings to the development of an idea. It is the collective wisdom that elicits the best results. The best ideas are often where we least expect them, so make it easy for everyone to be heard.

3. **Curiosity did not kill the cat.** In fact, it opened its mind and de-escalated conflict. Things will go wrong; mistakes will be made, and deadlines will be missed. We're human, busy with conflicting priorities and hit with externalities we didn't see coming. Avoid blame and finger pointing at all costs. This type of behaviour will only create defensiveness and long-term disengagement. Instead, become curious and engage in exploratory conversations to get to the root of an issue rather than assuming you already know the answer. I always coach innovation teams that the person who is responsible for the issue is usually the person who knows how to unlock the solution. It's our job to support, guide, and lean in to create a positive outcome.

Always remember, if you believe you know what the other person is thinking you're not ready to have a conversation.

4. **Authentic feedback.** Feedback can be good and bad, and we often need to have some difficult conversations. We all have blind spots and weaknesses in how we show up to work. Asking for feedback on your work, delivery, and ability to engage effectively enhances the communication between team members and supports the development of trust. When you do this – and only ever do this in an authentic and genuine manner – with people outside your team or your opponent (you know, the person who's not keen on the innovation project but you need their support) it disarms them, often turning a closed conversation into an open, two-way dialogue.

5. **It's a game of chess, so make sure you're thinking three moves ahead.** The purpose of this is to put the innovation team in the shoes of their internal decision-maker to pre-empt the information and content they will need along the entire innovation journey. By supporting their needs with context, information, and scenarios, we can help remove the ego and position-driven responses. Remember, this is a marathon and not a sprint, so move through this process with all your stakeholders with a supportive, thoughtful and considered approach.

HANDLING INHUMAN RESOURCES (AKA PASSIVE AGGRESSIVE BEHAVIOUR)

We've all been on the receiving end of this. Sadly, it's something I see in every organisation, and commonly it shows up with an 'us and them' mentality between those who are working in an innovation team and those who are not. Depending on which organisation, and on which day, both sides are equally guilty for their passive aggressive barbs and blockages.

I don't need to get into the detail of these behaviours. But we do need to call such behaviour out and manage it positively. Rolling our eyes and allowing others to behave this way or – worse – bitching about the situation to our colleagues ensures that we are perpetuating the problem because we are participating in it.

So, what do we do? In my experience, passive aggressive behaviour emerges on innovation teams when an individual or group of people either really want in on the idea (there's a touch of the green-eyed monster) or they genuinely believe it's a complete waste of time and can never add any value. In both of these scenarios, the best thing you can do is bring those people in to the inner circle and make them a part of your team or someone you consistently seek feedback from. This isn't a case of keeping your enemies closer; quite the opposite. These people have a significant amount of value to add and it needs to be harnessed.

When you have someone who is really opposed to an idea, instead of trying to overlook their passive aggressive behaviour, ask the person to join the team so you can hear their reasons. Don't just provide lip service to their ideas; rather, you need to really hear what their points are, because this is the true resistance you will probably also face with other people in the organisation. By understanding and digging right into the problem, you can see if you can solve it. It will slow you down and shift your focus away from what's really important, unless you manage it.

Understanding the real cause of the behaviour

I see this regularly at the senior leadership table when an idea is presented that may have been discussed or considered in previous years. In one of the financial institutions I have consulted to, there was an executive who was hell bent on stopping the investigation into a new idea that seemed to have considerable merit for the organisation. Interestingly, the potential development and implementation of this idea wouldn't have an impact on his division. The team and I were perplexed at his extremely vocal opposition and inability to support the idea, despite it requiring neither budget nor resources from his division.

Having an open conversation with the executive didn't shed a great deal of light on the situation, other than to understand this idea had been investigated a few years earlier. Yes, this idea review was done by this executive and his team. So, I did a bit more digging. The work completed by his team showed that this idea would not be viable due to the anticipated cost, internal capability, and risk of utilising untested and unknown technology. That all made perfect sense and sounded very reasonable – at the time.

But time moves on and things change. It was sensible to have another look at the development of this type of idea and reassess its viability for the organisation.

What's the real issue here? In this situation there was a deep fear of a loss of face and a perception that he got it wrong for not recommending this idea years earlier. I advised the team to take the approach of working with his team and understanding the work that had been done previously, and if appropriate, to bring any of these individuals into the team to support the work.

Sometimes it feels like it will be easier to climb K2 than it will be to get an extremely vocal executive to change their position. And be prepared for them *not* to change. In this instance, I advised the team to recognise the work completed earlier and validate that at the original point in time it was not right for the organisation to press ahead with that idea. All that information gave the innovation team a point of comparison to show the progressions which had occurred in the market, the cost differences, and the reasons why it needed to be reconsidered.

It's important to understand that leaders and individuals can, at times, feel threatened by innovation projects that they perceive should have been initiated by them. It's understandable. I am not saying it will be easy, but be inclusive where possible, and always remember it's about the work and not the person. Innovation always tends to throw up emotional responses from people inside the organisation. There are days when I feel more like a counsellor than a consultant. Don't brush off those moments or avoid them. Those tough conversations can help guide, focus, and channel passion into the right areas.

The other side is equally as problematic, and that's passive aggressive behaviour within innovation teams. This shows up in many ways, but the most common I see are:

- superiority

- exclusion

- resisting outside ideas

- blaming others if an idea or project isn't successful.

These behaviours impact the way the entire organisation views innovation, and how they will participate, support, and embrace it as a culture. Why would people want to participate in a culture that behaves that way? They won't, so rip it out from the roots and make it known there will be zero tolerance for that behaviour.

No matter where the passive aggressive behaviour stems from, as a collective we need to address it and have zero tolerance for it. Over time it will undermine the great work and potential successes of any projects. The success of innovation isn't just for the innovation team, but for the collective whole.

AVOIDING EXCLUSION AND SECRECY

Innovation managers are often seen as the cool kids. Sitting around on their beanbags, listening to binaural beats while they brainstorm in theta focus mode, playing ping-pong and constantly staring at walls of post-it notes. I say this tongue in cheek of course, but there really is an image and perception of being part of the elite few that some (not all) innovation teams portray. When I see this, I know they have become caught up in the hype of their own ideas or they have misunderstood what their role should be.

In one organisation I have worked with, innovation was the sole and exclusive job of one person. One person? That's crazy, and very myopic. This person's whole job and annual performance was based on how much revenue they were able to generate through innovative projects. I was really puzzled by this. Do they really want to operate in a bubble of one to look at future innovative opportunities? When I got into deep discussion with the leadership team, it became apparent that this was what some of the executives wanted but not others.

So, what happened? It turns out this organisation may have only had one official innovation 'guru', but in reality they had four other unofficial teams delivering their version of innovation. None of these areas spoke to each other, nor did they collaborate on the conceptual development and implementation of ideas. Rather, they tried to surprise and impress each other – and their bosses – once a project was up and running. I call this game 'my division is better than yours'. A little old-school business culture of divisional competition to supposedly drive up performance. Didn't work then, and it doesn't work today.

This culture of exclusion and secrecy is clearly driven from the top down, and it creates an internal competitiveness that's more cannibalistic than an infinite driver of success. Having different innovation agendas in the organisation doesn't lead to efficiency, collaboration, or a culture of success. Innovation by its very nature needs to be inclusive and collaborative. We'll dig into this later with some strategies on how to make this happen.

When innovation is done by only a few and others are excluded, you can expect the rest of the organisation to disengage. On a number of occasions I have seen employees become so frustrated and disenfranchised by the process that they have left the organisation to pursue the idea that no one would listen to and turn it into a successful business. The tools, access, and ability to have a side hustle are so easy these days, so you have to expect that if you are not listening and supporting your employees, they'll find a way to do it themselves. Remember, if you don't listen to your employees, you will end up with an organisation of people with nothing to say.

My favourite example of this still makes me giggle every time I think of it. There were a number of operational employees in a large infrastructure firm who identified a process and mechanism to make their job easier and more efficient. For years they pitched their idea to management and lobbied to get money in the annual planning process. While the idea was considered good, it was never taken seriously or given the go ahead. But, given the regulations in the industry, it should have been seen as a no-brainer. You may be able to guess what happened next – the team left the organisation, took a risk, and built a SaaS (software as a service) product to do exactly what they were asking the organisation to do.

Given their in-depth knowledge of the problem, their understanding of the machinations of the industry, and the recruitment of some gun IT dudes, they developed a program that has become the gold standard for that industry. Not only do they sell and operate this SaaS product with clients all around the world, they also sell this back to the organisation that didn't listen to them.

While not every idea will be as successful as this, and some will fail, imagine if that organisation had built that solution in-house as requested? That IP and revenue could have been part of that organisation.

What ideas are you missing by not listening to your employees?

CREATING A TOLERANCE FOR FAILURE

A key issue I encounter a lot is a zero tolerance for failure. This is the wrong way to look at innovation. What we need to have zero tolerance for is sloppy thinking, bad management, inconsistent approaches, and not putting the best technical skills on the idea development teams. Failing in a highly disciplined and transparent process will teach you more than you will ever learn from success.

No one wants to fail. Your employees certainly do not volunteer for an innovation program with the hope of it failing, but innovation is not without a high degree of uncertainty. It's important to be wary of failure, but we have to be able to distinguish between failing through incompetence and not being able to make an idea viable despite having a well-defined process, hardworking teams, and access to resources.

What we need is a zero-tolerance approach to incompetence. All innovation frameworks and cultures will have their share of failures.

Innovation is a risky business, and generally the corporate environment doesn't reward failure. Of any kind. Failure can be misinterpreted as laziness or incompetence.

It sounds obvious that innovation will entail a degree of failure, risk and uncertainty, something many organisations talk about failing forward with, but they don't really implement. That's all it is: talk. It often boils down to the performance metrics of employees. They do not have the ability to distinguish between a productive failure that is based on competent work, high standards, and a diligent 'learn as you go' methodology, compared to a failure that is based on bad management, poorly thought-out concepts, limited analysis, and a lack of transparency.

Instead of fearing failure, a different mindset needs to be adopted to build in mechanisms, feedback loops, and knowing when you may need to pull the pin on a project. Not being able to successfully prove a hypothesis through an innovation incubation process should not be perceived as a failure if a structured and supported process was followed.

If you fear failure and are seeking 100% certainty then you have to consider if innovation is right for you.

* * *

I'm not saying any of this to demonise innovation managers or teams. Quite the opposite. I understand the difficulties and challenges of creating and building corporate innovation ecosystems, and my team and I face these challenges on a daily basis. I am suggesting there's an alternative way forward. Before you can get your Corporate Innervation Operating System really humming along, you have to recognise these traits, behaviours, and problems to ensure you don't fall into these traps. You have to ask yourself, what culture do you really want inside your organisation, and do you really want to have an innovation ecosystem?

I know you always want to be on the right side of innovation, so in order to have a culture that doesn't tolerate these behaviours:

1. Build a culture of psychological safety to create the space for everyone to share, discuss, and contribute to ideas. Criticism, conflict, and opinions that destabilise the process will unfortunately be inevitable, but tackle it with a supportive, thoughtful, and considered approach.

2. Make it clear that there is a zero-tolerance approach to passive aggressive behaviour in the Corporate Innervation Operating System.

3. Remove the veil of exclusivity and open up the process for everyone to participate in. Innovation is the responsibility of everyone, and not a small, select group of people.

4. Don't fear failure if it occurs in a well-defined, structured process. Nurture a mindset and culture of considered thought and transparency, and learn through the process.

Why corporate innovation so often fails

Eliminate short-term thinking to move into the
long game of innovation.

We want it, talk about it, make it a value, and aspire to a culture of innovation. So why, then, if corporate innovation is something that almost 90% of mid to large organisations have as one of their values, strategies, or aspirational targets, are they not more successful at it?

This chapter is focused on highlighting the key reasons corporate innovation programs fail. We really need to confront these myths head on to debunk them because we don't want this to be us. What I am about to share with you happens in every leadership team, in every organisation, everywhere, at some point. It can only be tackled and resolved if we confront it head on and call it out in a thoughtful and constructive manner.

There's no shortage of tools, accelerator programs, and external courses to create innovation frameworks and come up with the next game-changing idea. So why do less than 5% of organisations have an innovation program that not only creates a sustainable culture of innovation inside the organisation, but also adds value to the bottom line with ideas that create tangible benefits?

There are five key reasons that corporate innovation programs fail:

1. Looking backwards instead of forward.

2. Short-term thinking.

3. Inertia: it looks like we're doing innovation but nothing changes.

4. Leadership that doesn't support innovation.

5. Attack of the energy vampires.

Let's have a look at each of these.

LOOKING BACKWARDS INSTEAD OF FORWARD

This is a tough one because in my experience it's very obvious to an outside consultant and the worker bees of the organisation but very difficult for the internal leaders to acknowledge. The answer to this is generally something that no one wants to hear, and it makes leaders squirm in their chairs a bit. The hard reality is that organisations are often stuck in the strategies, thinking, and processes which made them successful in the past that may no longer be relevant. With shareholders and boards in mind, executives and leadership teams often sell a strategy that's easy to digest, keeps the financials on target, and doesn't create too many waves. I know that is over-simplifying the issue, but there is often a 'steady as she goes' approach.

It's easy and comfortable to look through the lens of old and ignore new ideas, concepts, and processes, even if they did originate inside the organisation. The result is people with new ideas are told to assimilate and conform with the current way of thinking and 'how we do things around here', or innovation is externalised completely into an outside process. Either way, innovation is the ultimate loser.

SHORT-TERM THINKING

Unfortunately, strategy and leadership are often like politics and they play out in much the same way. It really is the dilemma of executives in all industries and organisations; in doing the groundwork, hard yards, and unheralded tasks of building and implementing long-term strategies, it will likely be their successors who reap the rewards. Couple this with the pressure to show results year on year and we end up with short-termism.

Innovation is a long-term play, and for many in the corporate environment it can be difficult to play the long game when results are required each year to show progress. For example, there is a desire to run 12-week accelerator or incubator programs and to be able to show some type of return on the investment for this time and resources. This can be almost impossible to predict unless the ideas are known prior to inception or are low-hanging fruit. But is it really innovation when we do this?

Delayed gratification of results is not something often rewarded by shareholders and the market. CEOs and C-suite executives find the dichotomy of current expectations and delayed results challenging. They are stuck in the quagmire of quarterly reporting cycles, annual performance requirements, and short-term pay incentives. It can be difficult to justify the short-term pain of an innovation portfolio that is not achieving quick and tangible results.

By avoiding the difficult task of operationalising a long-term plan for innovation and the development of a portfolio, we tend to avoid the traditional landmines of the corporate landscape. But we need to understand the long-term roadmap for innovation and future value creation, and provide an understanding of the journey the portfolio is taking. This is never going to be easy. Shareholders and markets are like addicts: they're constantly looking for a quick hit. This drives the incentive to deliver quick wins.

Boards have the responsibility to define the long-term strategic growth of the organisation and incentivise the CEO towards the desired behaviours. To achieve long-term success, incentive schemes for leaders and employees in the business need to draw out the right types of behaviours and focus on the development of a balanced portfolio, and where appropriate, allow for 'hockey stick' growth patterns. Good things come to those who put in the systems, processes, and ability to diligently work through ideas for long-term success.

Successful corporate innovation requires planning, skill, and – of course – some luck. It's not something you can wish for or mandate. You need to provide the training and support for leaders and doers alike to ensure they are supported and guided through the process of embedding innovation.

INERTIA: IT LOOKS LIKE WE'RE DOING INNOVATION BUT NOTHING CHANGES

Let's tackle the issue of inertia. This is an age-old problem with new programs, processes, and different ways of doing things in any workplace.

There will always be those enthusiastic bunnies who jump right into the deep end, boots and all, and just go for it. I love these people! But this is often a small minority of people who have either been gasping for a new way of doing things or are passionate about innovation. Others will be slower or more hesitant.

While there are often great intentions of building an innovative way of working, if it's not implemented correctly and enforced positively there can be inertia. Change is hard, and there will always be people who resist and dig into doing things the way they've always done them. You can find yourself pushing uphill against corporate values, culture, processes, and systems.

The sometimes excessive accountability culture of organisations means they're looking to dot every 'i' and cross every 't' for the monthly, quarterly, and annual reports. Innovation is messy, time-consuming, and it doesn't fit neatly into a planning and budgeting box. It is this ambiguity and sometimes inability to provide an exact answer that creates inertia and slows down progress.

LEADERSHIP THAT DOESN'T SUPPORT INNOVATION

An innovation culture needs to be led from the top down. And not just in a way that provides lip service and a box-ticking approach.

Let me provide you with a seemingly benign but really common example that I see in almost every workplace I have consulted to: the problem of meetings. This is a problem in so many ways for people of all levels inside organisations. And it seems to be something that is very difficult to get the right balance on.

We often have too many meetings. This can occur for a variety of reasons, including lack of clarity, trying to consult with too many people, poor processes, and paralysis by analysis.

It's really common – and probably quite the trend – to have the rules of engagement for meetings plastered all over the walls of meeting rooms. I always find this fascinating, because it seems there's been a decision made somewhere that not only will the people of the organisation take these rules on by osmosis, but the more senior you are the more the rules do not apply. You've seen it, and been impacted by it: your meeting starts 15 minutes late because the meeting before you overran, and it was filled with senior leaders, so they made the people who had the room booked wait … and wait. Or worse still, they've asked the next meeting attendees to find another room.

You might say, *hang on a minute, their meeting was important and they needed to finalise some outcomes for a key project.* Sure, I have no doubt it was really important. And this may seem like a really trivial example, but that's the point. It says to do as I say but not as I do. If we want something to work and be effective, *all* members of the organisation have to participate. The role of leaders is even more important in that they need to drive the change from the top down and lead by example.

How does this relate to innovation? The creation of a real innovation culture that works requires the ongoing ability of leaders to support it, even if they are not actively participating in a live innovation project. Team members look to their leaders for guidance, support, and confirmation they're on the right track.

ATTACK OF THE ENERGY VAMPIRES

I love this term, and I really wish I was the person who came up with this phrase. If you're not familiar with this term, you will be familiar with these people in the workplace. These are the people in an organisation who suck the energy right out of the room when they come in. It might seem overly dramatic, but I feel like I can see the creativity and ideas leave the room when these people join a meeting. It's almost like the lights dim a little bit. It can suck the life and soul right out of an innovation project. This shows up in many forms, but I regularly see it in the forms of backchanneling, non-constructive criticism, blockages, and protectionism.

You have probably come across these people throughout your career; I know I have. In the innovation space, if you have people who are influential and are energy vampires you can almost guarantee people will not stick their neck out with new ideas, for fear of what will happen next, whether that be in the form of negative feedback, killing the idea, taking credit for the idea to boost their career, or taking a destructive form of control. While these people may not actually be taking blood, they are draining their teams and people of energy, motivation and confidence in their abilities, leaving them unable and not wanting to provide new ideas and participate in innovation.

I'm sure we can all share stories about energy vampires in the workplace, but one that I use to illustrate this is Gordon Gekko from the movie *Wall Street*. He was a well-known character for his dubious morals and catchcry of 'greed is good'. Gordon comes across as powerful, charismatic, dynamic, hungry for success, and is described in the movie as the 'guy who had an ethical bypass at birth'. If you haven't seen this movie I recommend that you do. This is a man who has no shame corrupting his protégé, manipulating him, and getting him to do his dirty work. His only interest is doing things that helped himself, and damn the consequences for anyone else.

This is a caricature to showcase the shameless villainy, moral ambivalence, and narcissistic behaviour that can raise its ugly head in the corporate world. Luckily, this extreme case is just a fictional character, but it's important to understand that energy vampires will show up in many and varied forms.

The nature of innovation tends to attract those who are charismatic, and they may initially appear to be a tornado of energy and ideas. This can attract people to them like moths to the flame. But, it's important to remember the role of your innovation leaders isn't to elevate their own position and ideas, it's to develop, nurture, and mentor the people inside your organisation. The Corporate Innervation Operating System is about the development of your people, unlocking their genius and developing a culture of innovation.

If you have leaders in the organisation who are energy vampires, you can guarantee their teams are not going to support the process by providing or developing any ideas.

* * *

I will provide you with a process and tools to support the constructive development of innovation teams and a culture for success. If you support it and positively fight for it, it can be like a stream of water and flow through the entire business as employees take their learnings and new ways of working back to their business-as-usual teams and adapt it for their own success.

In the short term, you can achieve some quick wins to progress the development of innovation inside your organisation:

1. Have an open mind about what you will do to create success in the future. It's time to stop deferring to doing what you have always done because it's safe and comfortable. Be brave, and only use the retrospective lens for context and understanding of what you have done in the past.

2. Eliminate short-term thinking to move into the long game of innovation. You are not looking to be a one-hit wonder with a single idea. The focus should be on building a long-term portfolio – the expectation of instantaneous results needs to be removed.

3. Remove the inertia that's often coupled with innovation, where there is a lot of talk and intention, but nothing really changes. It is crucial not to snap back into the old ways to ensure you maintain motivation and momentum with your team.

4. Ensure your leadership team is fully on board and supporting innovation. This is more than a tick-the-box exercise: there is an energy shift that needs to occur so that you have everyone in the organisation walking the talk … and not just talking about it.

5. Cut the energy vampires out of your innovation process. Be ruthless to ensure that you are building and nurturing a culture of growth, development, and open dialogue to progress ideas.

6

Common innovation myths

Innovation is an attitude that's almost impossible
to achieve through process alone.

Corporate Innervation is a culture, a lifestyle, a way of thinking, and a holistic belief that your people are your best innovation assets. If you want to be effective in this space you need to unshackle yourself from the myths that are holding you back. Innovation is hard enough; don't make it harder by creating additional barriers and hurdles for your people to get it right. We shackle ourselves enough in the corporate world in the form of processes, reporting, and methodologies ... it's time to take the gloves off and change the neural pathways of the organisation to embed a Corporate Innervation process that works.

Innovation is *not* a process or a method. This may be the biggest myth of corporate innovation. It cannot be a 'build it and it will come' mentality. It's more than an attitude and is almost impossible to achieve through process alone.

Innovation is a way of thinking based on managing uncertainty, intuitively reading the signals in the market, a whole lot of gut instinct, and tenacity. To innovate you must be willing to work with and through the uncertainty, be willing to work through the potential failures, changes, trial and error, and rethinking required to deliver a successful idea. It will never be a neat strategy that can be delivered within acceptable tolerances to the budget. The rewards will always be commensurate with the risk undertaken to get there. If we truly want to innovate and find the genius inside the organisation, we need to change our attitude towards corporate innovation.

But before we can rethink corporate innovation, we need to debunk the myths, remove all of the theatre of innovation, and get rid of the barriers, real and perceived, that are holding organisations back. Innovation by its very nature is about challenging the status quo, driving change for growth and building opportunities that deliver value to the bottom line. Interestingly, many innovation ecosystems are stymied by the very people we look to for delivery of these frameworks.

There are many myths and barriers to corporate innovation. I'm going to go through the ones I see on a regular basis – the ones that really stop the development of corporate innovation ecosystems, and are why many innovation programs fail to deliver value to the bottom line. These myths are:

1. Innovation can only be done by those selected in the organisation.

2. A boring problem begets a boring solution.

3. Innovation is business improvement.

4. Innovation must be disruptive.

5. Innovation is a top-down-only approach.

6. Innovation is predictable.

7. Innovation is a solo activity.

8. Everybody loves innovative change.

9. We are Agile and that makes us innovative.

10. Innovation just happens.

MYTH: INNOVATION CAN ONLY BE DONE BY THOSE SELECTED BY THE ORGANISATION

Many organisations set aside a strategy or innovation team (sometimes both) to be the chosen few who get to look at innovation opportunities for the organisation. The organisation looks to these people to be the visionaries and shining light for all innovation ideas and opportunities. Often, this will be directed from a top-down approach where the strategic vision for the next three to five years is being considered and there are some gaps in the defined programs and initiatives that have been selected by the leadership and strategy teams. These teams will often employ a methodical approach to thinking, using a process such as design thinking, double-diamond, or something similar to really understand the problem, consider a number of different opportunities, and come up with an 'innovative' solution. This process often uses the same people who came up with the strategy containing the gaps in the first place.

The problem here is neither the methodology being used nor the people in the team. I have no doubt that such people are usually intelligent and great at their job. The problems are:

1. The concept of 'innovate on demand' and using a closed group of people to think through a much broader problem. This black-box thinking approach means you are using a limited number of minds that may be fatigued by the strategic business planning process.

2. Thinking that innovation operates at the same speed and timing as the strategic planning process.

Knowing that boards, CEOs, and executive leadership teams all want a degree of certainty for their strategy, this creates a requirement to fill all the 'gaps' and doesn't leave much room for future change. This moves through the mechanical process of defining and delivering the strategy, defining the high-level programs of work to deliver the strategy and operational requirements, budgeting, and prioritisation. It rolls on from there into a structured and defined series of portfolios and programs of work that have been agreed upon to achieve the goals of the organisation.

Then there's the budgeting process, which is often more like horse trading, and this results in trade-offs, bargaining, delays, budget cuts, reduced scopes of work and … I could keep going … but this isn't about the game theory of corporate strategy and budgeting, it's about creating an innovation framework that creates value.

One of the organisations I have spent considerable time working with and building a culture of innovation in has opened up their thinking to the ability to leave gaps and areas for movement in the top-down strategic process. Building in an openness to accept some gaps will create an opportunity to run a series of discovery processes to consider solutions that will provide real value. This also creates an opportunity to pivot, fail, or not pursue a given option.

You need to think of this as a two-speed process, where the overarching strategy of the organisation is the slow, steady, and known component, and innovation is the ad-hoc, undefined idea that cannot be locked down on a planning calendar. When we try to put innovation into a defined box, we are going to miss the ideas and opportunities that turn up when we least expect it. As is the nature of innovation.

We don't know what we don't know. And you also can't be expected to have a perpetual planning cycle. Be open to the concept that ideas will float up outside the planning and budget process and cycle. Don't defer them or put them off to the next 'planning season'. Make sure your portfolios of work are so incredibly robust that you are able to assess these ideas against the current and planned work to make an immediate strategic decision on what to do with an idea. It doesn't make sense to delay an idea that may provide a better outcome for the organisation because you need to stick with your current plan. Look, I know as well as any other executive that this is easier said than done. I have a process for this in the Corporate Innervation Operating System, because – while this sounds easy in theory – it's challenging to implement.

MYTH: A BORING PROBLEM BEGETS A BORING SOLUTION

I often see the expectation that innovation has to be exciting and disruptive. There is a mindset among a lot of people that innovation is always digital, a technical transformation, or disruptive.

An organisation I have spent some time advising had these types of phrases painted in huge letters in a mural on their wall, and a reference of what not to do throughout their 'innovation framework'. I almost spat out my coffee the first time I saw this. They are an organisation lamenting the poor progress of their innovation program, yet they can't understand that they're telling their people they don't want to hear from them unless they have an earth-shattering idea. It's a great way to shut down the voices of your employees.

I see this a lot in the organisations I work with that are frustrated with a lack of results or ability to engage their people in innovation. I also know that when I see this type of rhetoric about innovation in an organisation, it has been driven by ego and a misunderstanding of the strategic objectives of the organisation. Seeing this, I know I have to go back to the beginning of the process and help them start again to guide them through a process that will add real value, because if you're not doing this with your innovation program then … why are you doing it?

Telling the organisation *'a boring problem begets a boring solution'* is ensuring the employees of that organisation vet their ideas before they talk to their teams or leaders about them. The true value of innovation is lost if the organisation is infatuated with bright, shiny ideas. It's often the innovations that *don't* have the instant wow factor that create the most value to the bottom line. The genius is often in the simple things that no one thinks about because they are too simple.

Great innovation can be boring

Breville is a great example of a company that recognises innovation can be boring, unsexy, and sometimes go unnoticed, but if it makes a significant difference to the customer experience and in return the bottom line, that is a huge success for the company. Aren't sales and customer experience more important than wow factor?

In the 1980s, Breville invented the Assist Plug, which looks like a basic loop at the back of a plug to help you push it in and pull it out of the wall more easily. The idea came from some customer feedback saying the plugs 'take some force to remove'. Considerable thought went into this problem. Breville looked at data on the size of human fingers, created a number of prototypes and trials, and worked out that to make it work and be easy, the hole needed to accommodate the finger between the first and second knuckle. Once they got this right then the team went through more protypes and trials for comfort. Being the only company with a plug like this, they were able to patent it in 2002, which is why you've probably never seen another plug quite like it on a competitor product.

The usability and comfort of the Assist Plug was loved so much by customers that Breville started to incorporate it into many aspects of their product designs, from blender lids to steam wands on coffee machines. This became a significant competitive advantage for Breville. The Assist Plug was such an incredible success that it was even included as part of their logo for a number of years.

In more recent times, Breville ran into a problem of toast cooking differently in Australia than it did in America. It turns out that the different voltage and sugar quantities in bread created different outcomes for the customer. To arrest their falling sales and market share, solutions needed to be considered, and this required getting a deep understanding of the food supply chain and the impact of the different voltage requirements. Again, Breville spent a significant amount of time investigating solutions to find the perfect piece of toast. Mornings can be hard enough; great toast can make someone's day a little bit smoother.

Let's be honest; there's nothing sexy about fingerloops on plugs or getting the perfect shade of brown on toast. But they are pragmatic, usable solutions that create real ongoing value to Breville not only through creating a better product but also through a better customer experience, which creates loyal customers. They speak to the understanding in the ecosystem that there are no boring ideas, just opportunities to look at how they can improve the customer experience through great design.

A number of challenges arise from the mindset that boring problems only create boring solutions, most importantly the belief that a person's idea will not be good enough or different enough. Most employees have really big workloads, and are focused on managing their day-to-day tasks and ensuring they meet their performance requirements, often only taking the time to consider new ideas in their free time. If only the sexy and disruptive ideas are considered, why would the people in the organisation continue to share their knowledge and use their time to consider ideas that are never acknowledged? This provides the appearance that management and the senior leadership team can tick the box and consider the business innovative. This becomes a disincentive to participate.

True innovation needs to be focused on what creates the best outcomes for the organisation, its internal and external customers, and not necessarily on the sexy ideas. And it takes a brave soul to tell an executive leadership team that the sexy, disruptive, and PR-grabbing ideas won't be the ones that solve their customer pain points and create value on the bottom line. Delivering emerging technologies and bleeding-edge solutions are often attractive for innovation managers and leadership teams to define their legacy, but is this providing the outcomes and experiences the customers really want? While we should never rule out the need for a deep and transformative innovation if it suits the business, we should not take our attention off solving the critical, and often boring, problems for the organisation.

MYTH: INNOVATION IS BUSINESS IMPROVEMENT

A common misconception is that innovation and the process to develop ideas can be used for the development of a continuous improvement process. Unfortunately, innovation and business improvement are often words that are used interchangeably, and it makes people like me cry a little on the inside every time. We often see titles like 'Innovation and Improvement Team' or 'Continuous Improvement and Innovation Team', and it's clear the organisation is unsure of the purpose, remit, and goals of these teams.

An innovation portfolio is the place for wicked problems, new, creative and on occasion, disruptive ideas. The purpose of innovation is to do something new in order to grow, maintain your position in the market, or keep step with your competitors.

Business improvement is looking at your current processes or how something is done and seeing if you can make it better, more efficient, or more effective. The purpose is to maximise the utility of the resources allocated or available. As Kaizen, Six Sigma and other devotees will attest to, what you are looking for here is to refine a process as much as possible to reduce costs and inefficiencies.

Can business improvement and innovation overlap? Sure, at the heart of it, but innovation must add value.

Innovation can be a slow burn that moves through an incremental development process. Many great innovations are based on step changes and improvements. Most of the technology we see and use today is the result of incremental innovation, and some of this may not be enough to attract huge amounts of attention but will still provide material impacts to the bottom line.

How you share your innovation mission with your organisation and employees will determine the outcomes. The one thing you should absolutely avoid is attempting to apply continuous improvement to innovation. An innovation idea can't be regimented, nor should it be controlled in the early stages. Ideas need room to grow, evolve, and mature into something that you are able to make an informed decision on. Innovation struggles to survive in an environment of continuous improvement because it doesn't fit into a neat little predefined box that you happen to have room for in your strategy and budget.

MYTH: INNOVATION MUST BE DISRUPTIVE

We are not in a disrupt-or-die environment. This comes back to the purpose and vision for innovation. Do you want to create a process for longevity and evolution with your current and future customers? Or are you harbouring a secret burning desire to run a startup in the safety net of a corporate environment? It is too easily forgotten that disruption starts with unhappy customers.

Being disruptive is the badge that many Innovation Managers and Leaders want to wear. Disruption occurs when an innovation develops a new market, resulting in a new business model that causes your competitors or other established players to lose market share or fail.

In any strategy, leadership and brainstorming discussion, disruption is thrown around and can often feel a bit threatening. Boards and leadership teams are asked to be vigilant and defend against disruption, and it seems some can get caught in the trap that the only way to grow is to disrupt their own industry.

Innovation is not synonymous with disruption. In many instances in a corporate environment a disruptive innovation will inevitably cannibalise another area or division of the organisation.

Disruption often sees an organisation try to make the new idea fit into the old business model, which not only fails as establishing the best way to develop in the new market but also neglects the old markets.

Non-disruptive creation is exciting, challenging, and the stuff that makes me leap out of bed every morning. These are the real problem-solving opportunities that allow organisations to create new markets without destroying a current one. This removes the mindset that we are playing a zero-sum game, and moves us into an infinite mindset where innovation is creative and not destructive.

One of my favourite examples of non-disruptive creation is *Sesame Street* in 1969, and I love it because not only did it create a new market for pre-school edutainment, it is still shown in over 147 countries in 30 languages. I watched it, my daughter watched it, and we can all relate to Big Bird, Oscar the Grouch, Elmo or whoever was your favourite character teaching us the word, letter and number of the day.

Sesame Street wasn't designed to replace early childhood education, rather it was designed to help children prepare for school. The goal of the original producer Joan Ganz Cooney was 'to create a children's television show that would master the addictive qualities of television and do something good with them'. What resulted was a show that children loved to watch and didn't even realise they were learning. What seemed like the antithesis of education, created an entire industry that is now known as edutainment that contributes to the educational development of our children without replacing schools, books, libraries or the time parents spend reading with their children.

MYTH: INNOVATION IS A TOP-DOWN APPROACH ONLY

Innovation doesn't come from the boardroom, executive teams, or the management table. So, stop forcing it to be driven from there. The board and executives are responsible for the strategic direction of the organisation. This will absolutely provide opportunities and direction for the whole of the organisation to be guided by and participate in ideas and solutions to fill the many holes that will inevitably occur.

An innovation framework, like strategy, is only as good as its implementation, and the people executing it. The critical success factors will be:

- Do all the people in your organisation understand the vision, purpose, and goals of the innovation framework?

- Will they buy into it and participate in the process?

- Have you provided your people with the skills, tools, resources, coaches, and guidance to make it happen?

Innovation comes from the people who know the customers well, both internal and external, and understand what they want. It comes when there is a push from the bottom up of ideas to fill the gaps and change the culture of innovation inside your organisation.

Corporate Innervation is where amazing innovation happens inside the organisation. It is the intersection of the future strategy and collective wisdom of the people of the organisation. The vision of implementing the Corporate Innervation Operating System is for the people of your organisation to own innovation, so that there will be alignment between the top down and bottom up to maximise the outcomes for innovation.

MYTH: INNOVATION IS PREDICTABLE

Let's be honest … innovation is messy, unpredictable, challenging, and almost impossible to plan for. We just don't know when the next little brain explosion is going to occur which can deliver a game-changing idea. Innovation is often a numbers game. Not every idea is going to work. Occasionally, but not often, we get an idea in the first five to come through the framework that shoots the lights out and provides a significant return on investment and creates budget to pay for the development of future ideas. This is the dream that all leadership teams are looking for: an immediate result. But innovation is a little like dating: you have to meet lots of people and kiss a few frogs before you find someone you want to settle in with.

The majority of corporate structures require strategic planning, budgeting, and management of the process to ensure the internal and external (if applicable) and shareholder requirements are met. This is generally the case for private and publicly listed companies and their requirement to operate within the interests of shareholders. It is this driving force that creates a tension between providing the maximum returns for shareholders in the short term and playing a long game to create and deliver programs of work that will provide solutions in future horizons but may not return value today.

In the corporate world we want to put everything in neat boxes and plan with as much detail as possible for the period ahead. We want to be able to forecast with a degree of certainty, and create meaningful targets for teams and key performance indicators that allow us to measure performance and in some instances decide on an annual bonus. Innovation by its very nature does not fit into these parameters of time or forecasting.

In the startup world, the investment hockey stick curve and uncertainty over future returns is a given. For some people it's part of the appeal, and for others it's a risk they are willing to take given their belief and willingness to commit to an outcome.

It's this uncertainty and degree of risk that makes many leaders and executives in the corporate environment go weak at the knees … and not in a good way. Not being able to define an outcome, forecast a return on investment, or in some instances have a basic understanding of whether an idea will even work, prohibits many leadership teams from feeling they can commit to a program of innovation or a particular idea.

I worked with an organisation that predefines the criteria for innovation success being able to provide an immediate return of $2m revenue in the first 12 months, or it is deemed unviable to even start the initial ideation and discovery process. Not a lot of scope for the development of unknown ideas there. The *real* innovation ideas. This locks the organisation into a predictable path for the future and doesn't provide for the capability to design, develop, and implement a variety of inward- and outward-facing ideas. If this criteria was applied to many of the organisations I have worked with and continue to work with, they would be missing out on many ideas that have created significant changes to the way they work and considerable value to the bottom line.

A game-changing innovation

With this attitude, Michael – an electrical maintenance officer at an airport – would not have been able to bring to life an idea that created efficiency, safety, and sustainability gains that make a $2m revenue target pale in comparison.

After an innovation workshop one day, Michael spoke to me about his idea. He had been sitting on this idea for years and had been unable to obtain an audience or any support for its development. I was blown away by the amount of research, time, and effort he had put into this idea. This was a man who was truly passionate about this idea and was willing to put in the hours at home to see if he could make it work. You can't buy this type of passionate employee.

Michael's challenge was based on developing a process and mechanism to clean the airport runway lights better. My curiosity levels were raised immediately – who doesn't want clean, bright, shiny airport runway lights (known as lenses) when their plane is coming into land at night? The thought of dull lights was making me feel a little anxious. If there's an airport runway light cleaner who doesn't think the lights are clean enough, I really want to hear what he has to say ...

Michael told me about the current practice, which is industry standard at many airports around the world. It requires a team of two or three maintenance officers and an airside officer guide to go out on the runaway at night (generally after 10 or 11pm) and work through the night to clean the lenses. To clean the lenses they have to get on their hands and knees and scrub them with steel wool and a chemical cleaner to remove the rubber and debris that builds up and sticks to the lenses. It is time consuming, dangerous and really, really hard on their bodies to be kneeling on the asphalt and scrubbing for hours.

I was gobsmacked and intrigued that such a technical and precise operation like an airport still required the runway lenses to be scrubbed by hand. He was also concerned that hand-scrubbing in a time-limited period meant the job wasn't being done very well. And this wasn't because they were lazy: it was difficult getting clearance from the tower to enter the runaway, scrub the lens, and do it in the time allotted by air traffic control.

Michael told me that his personal pride and that of his team was based on ensuring those lenses are the cleanest and brightest runway lenses. When you find employees like Michael, you know you've struck gold. (We'll talk about these types of employees and how to empower them later.) This pride in his work was making Michael question if there was a better way to do this.

After hours and hours of research and a few experiments at home, Michael came up with a conceptual idea based on a number of different methods being trialled in other airports and a focus on what will work in his environment. A plan was hatched. A pitch was created, and a conceptual design of a machine to undertake this work was created. The idea of a compressed bicarbonate of soda cleaning mechanism was born.

This idea was pitched at the senior management level to obtain budget and resource approval to move forward with the development of a proof of concept. It was an eye-opening experience for me – as I was pitching this idea on behalf of Michael – to realise the majority of these senior leaders didn't know the process that this team goes through to clean the lenses. The audible intake of breath when I explained the manual process, in addition to the safety, OH&S and environmental issues with the current process, made me realise I was providing them with new information. Only one leader in that team was aware of the process.

Given the nature of this idea, the senior leadership team saw this as a bit of a novelty, and with the small amount of money being requested for a proof of concept, the team agreed. After moving through all the correct risk, safety, governance, and environmental approvals, a small machine was developed to assess the feasibility of the idea.

The machine was tested in all conditions for a number of months, and the results were outstanding. The team could complete the task in half the time using half the people. In addition, a bag of bicarb to use in the machine costs approximately $25, and that's enough for one runway – significantly less than the cost of the chemicals. The proof of concept was such a success that we went on to get an industrial design for an automated machine that can be used by the driver without having to leave the vehicle.

This idea, while unable to generate revenue, was a game-changing innovation for the airport that created significant benefits to the bottom line via:

- efficiencies, through requiring 50% fewer staff to complete the cleaning

- less water usage

- reduced costs of chemicals.

And the other benefits to the organisation were greater than what hits the bottom line:

- happy staff who are proud of what they have achieved and what they do to keep the airport running

- encouraging openness to try an idea that makes it easier for someone to do their job, rather than just focusing on profit

- super-bright, sparklingly clean runway lenses.

This real-life example highlights that it's not always possible to plan the solution or understand the return on investment from the outset, but we can establish a predictable, standardised, and repeatable way of working to assess, decide, prioritise, and potentially test ideas.

MYTH: INNOVATION IS A SOLO ACTIVITY

People often think of innovation as something that smart, creative and in some instances solo geniuses do. But this really couldn't be further from the truth. It's the talent, hard work, and energy in a team that brings an idea to life. Innovation needs to be an inherent part of the culture, the organisational philosophy, and way of working. In my experience the real value often comes from outside the strategy and innovation teams, from the people who know the business, the gaps, and how they need something to work 'in the real world'.

I see this problem play out in two ways:

- the transference of an idea to an innovation manager for assessment, and if they like it then they complete all the work

- an individual digs in and works on an idea in isolation for fear of either not being in control of the idea or outcome or other people taking on the project and getting all the credit.

Both of these individualistic approaches will fail to provide the desired results. This attitude is something I move to disable really quickly when reviewing corporate innovation ecosystems.

The real role of the innovation manager or team inside an organisation is to be the guide, coach, and mentor for teams to build out ideas into a concept, and where appropriate through to build, implementation, and deployment. Sometimes one person may have an incredible brain explosion or thought bubble to create something or do something differently, but as a general rule it takes an entire team to bring an idea together.

As my late, great father taught me (as only a passionate teacher can), everything I do in both my academic and business career is because I am standing on the shoulders of giants. All the giant thinkers, researchers, doers, and people who have tried and failed and tried and succeeded – it is these people that we are learning from and growing from. What we do is the culmination of all the research, ideas, and effort of the people that have gone before us, and it's how we use this knowledge and package different ideas together that will create game-changing opportunities.

All too often I see in the corporate environment people seeking to claim credit and ownership of ideas to maximise their ability to navigate the political environment of the corporate jungle. It's often a polite 'lord of the flies' process that often sees the best players leave and take their ideas with them. Don't let your process devolve into something that resembles the survival of the fittest.

MYTH: WE ALL LOVE INNOVATIVE CHANGE

The hard truth about innovation is not everyone loves it, and it can be very difficult to get some people to come on the journey. My experience in coaching teams on innovation – from executive leadership teams to innovation delivery teams – is that innovation can create quite a strong emotional response in people, both positive and negative.

There is often the view that everyone should love innovation and get really excited about it. And a lot of people will, but you will also have a large number of people who feel connected to how they work and operate today, and don't see the reason for change. This resistance often comes from a place of the unknown; they don't have enough information to understand and visualise where this is going in the future. Or, through a process of fear where they may be excluded or worse off as a result of the implementation of an innovation program.

The reasons people don't like innovation or are resistant to it include:

- **There is low or no trust.** This happens when people have heard unfulfilled promises before or they don't believe the organisation will be able to deliver. There may also be some uncertainty around how their ideas will be viewed.

- **They feel it's a new trend and it will pass.** If your people think this is just a passing fad and it's not going to be a permanent part of the future, they are unlikely to put the effort in to participate.

- **They feel connected to the current way of doing things.** Your people are continually being asked to do something new or different, and this may just be the latest cab off the rank for them. In some instances, they're just hardwired to do things the way they know and are comfortable with.

- **They fear the unknown.** This is a fear that's not often admitted; some people feel that innovation may weaken or remove their position in the organisation.

- **They see no benefit to being involved.** *Why get involved when I can do my job, get paid, and go home without any extra stress or fuss?* This sounds like something you may expect to hear from lower level employees, but it's actually something I hear regularly from managers and leaders. Why? They already feel overwhelmed with performance and budget targets, so the thought of adding an unknown variable into this mix makes them want to run for the hills. If they don't do it, they can't fail and they can't be held accountable.

The biggest mistake will be to overlook any of the reasons, fears, or indicators of resistance and not proactively deal with them. Innovation needs to be led by the entire executive and leadership team. Don't leave it to the innovation manager alone. This is an open-ended process that you will continually need to work at to create a fundamental change and evolving culture of innovation.

MYTH: WE ARE 'AGILE' AND THAT MAKES US INNOVATIVE

For the purposes of this myth you can replace 'Agile' with any other way of working or project-management methodology. One of the things I often hear from managers and leadership teams is that 'they are Agile' and they 'are innovative' as a result. I do feel like I die a little on the inside every time I hear this. What I am challenged by is their inability to understand that innovation is the process of creating change, and being agile is their ability to adapt to change. At the heart of the methodology, no matter how you choose to employ it, Agile is a process to adopt continuous improvement and allow for positive change to occur through the development and deployment of projects.

Using an agile mindset or adapted methodology for development will not allow for the development of new ideas or be the driver of innovation and value creation. Agile is a fantastic methodology, and one that I love and use to implement systematic, repeatable processes that enable the opportunity to fail fast when designing and developing ideas. But it will not create a culture of innovation, a pipeline of ideas, or the ability to share inspiration. Employed correctly, it will support iterative prototyping and development to overcome the common problems of implementing successful innovations. As a way of working, it can be immensely successfully beyond the IT and innovation teams to support efficient delivery of work and consistent collaboration and transparency in all teams.

We have to be careful of subscribing to dogmas in relation to innovation. Initially the development of Agile involved a set of management practices to support the efficient and cost-effective development of software. This enabled continuous change and the ability to draw on the talents of collaborative teams to create a process that permitted projects and teams to move forward with uncertainty and volatility, allowing for just enough to be completed in each iteration to maximise outcomes and budgets and not go too far.

This is not a discussion to get rid of Agile. Quite the opposite. I'm a huge fan of Agile and similar methodologies. I teach them, and advocate for executive teams to implement these methodologies where it's appropriate for an organisation. The values, principles, and benefits are aligned with my way of thinking. But a delivery methodology that accommodates continuous change, continuous improvement, and the opportunity to fail fast if necessary will *not* create an innovation portfolio or a culture of innovation. It's just a system to be used *after* you already know exactly what you want to do.

A real innovation framework creates the space for exploration of new ideas, in all facets of the organisation, beyond the current program of work and strategy. Innovation is unplanned, chaotic, and challenges the status quo. Agile will not find the solution to the problem you didn't know existed, nor will it support the creation of additional value streams through non-disruptive creation. What it will do is help you deliver it ... once you know what 'it' is.

This is not about getting rid of Agile or whatever variation you are using inside your organisation. It's about understanding its purpose and place, and knowing what an Agile or Agile-style methodology will and will not do.

MYTH: INNOVATION JUST HAPPENS

Innovation doesn't happen by accident ... it happens by design. Enough said, right?

I wish this was clear, but it isn't. The problem is there is often a need to package innovation into a neat little defined program where each idea will take 6, 12 or however many weeks is defined by the process. The frustrating truth is that innovation takes as long as it takes. Sometimes that can be days or weeks, and in other instances years.

Innovation isn't the development of co-working spaces with ping-pong tables, beanbags, and matching T-shirts. It's the provision of mental space to develop, conceptualise, and mature ideas for the organisation.

When staff are overloaded with work they will be unable to consider new ideas, reflect on the process, or research any ideas they have floating around in their heads. Providing the mental space is something we don't talk about and assume it just happens. I'm not advocating that we provide 'special thinking time' or anything like that; I'm suggesting we get back to some excellent principals of leadership where we don't overload staff and instead keep their work levels sustainable.

* * *

In this chapter I have run through the top 10 myths that create a blockage or mental barrier to innovation in the corporate environment. For you to really implement a Corporate Innervation process, reflect on these and consider the impact on the mindset, culture, and process you may have in place:

- Think about the myths you are buying into, and challenge yourself and your team to remove them from the organisation. Treat it like a swear jar and get everyone to make a gold coin donation when they slip back into the old ways. You'll have a great donation for your chosen charity at the end of the year.

- Consider the current operations inside your organisation and how you can unwind some of the processes that may be blocking the future of innovation.

- Keep work at a sustainable level that doesn't make people feel consistently overloaded, to allow them the mental space to look at everything that's happening from their perspective and consider new ideas.

Why you have an innovation graveyard

Culture cannot be imported, copied, or borrowed.
It's an outcome of the systems, processes, and consistent
coaching and development of your people to build
an innovation culture.

SEVEN COMMON KILLERS OF INNOVATION

A fundamental element of the Corporate Innervation process is establishing a culture that supports creative thinking, the development of solutions, and is backed up by a framework and process. This is what most organisations are seeking, yet they inadvertently create an innovation graveyard because they can't break through ingrained habits and institutionalised processes that stifle creativity, block rational risk-taking, and disengage most people in the organisation.

What happens when your employees give you their ideas and nothing happens with them? You end up with an innovation graveyard. This is not only where your employees' ideas have gone to be buried and forgotten about, it's also where the soul of innovation in your organisation goes to die.

The quickest ways to kill an innovation program, or to have people in your organisation disengage from the process, are:

1. **Ignoring the ideas that are being provided from people in the organisation.** When employees provide you with their ideas for innovation and they are not acknowledged or reviewed, it's an indicator you have implemented an innovation program that is propped up with theatre.

2. **Never moving past the idea-gathering stage.** Whether this happens through the problem of paralysis by analysis, no time, or competing priorities, if you have taken the time to gather people's thoughts and ideas and they never hear anything more about it, they are likely to assume you either didn't value them or it was just an attempt at engagement.

3. **Defaulting to, 'No, but … '** This immediate reaction to ideas is common, and it is shrouded in the comfort of how we do things today and a myopic view of new ideas that sit a little left of centre. We need to be defaulting to a response of, 'Yes, and … ', to encourage creativity and an understanding that not every idea will be successful. Failure at some point is a certainty in innovation, but before any idea can be an overwhelming success it needs to start out as a crazy idea.

4. **Creating competition.** Nothing breaks the soul of an innovation culture more than competition between teams, divisions, or people inside an organisation. As I discussed earlier, the theatre of innovation often uses this as its basis. Collaboration, cross-pollination of ideas, and sharing information are some of the core elements of successful innovation. Without them, people are operating in silos and fostering a culture of protectionism.

5. **Only talking about innovation.** When leaders throw around the word 'innovation' and dot it through their strategy documents and business cases but don't follow it up with any action, it shows that no one is taking ownership of innovation or actively seeking to support new ideas.

6. **Punishing mistakes.** When we make people afraid of making mistakes or actively taking risks and they are punished if they fail, we kill innovation. People will never be motivated to participate if they must have a guaranteed winner. The Tata Group understand this, and acknowledged they needed to reframe their thinking if they were going to build a successful culture of innovation. They shifted their thinking and the language used in this space to create the 'Dare to Try' award. This award is presented to teams that have made an unsuccessful, but carefully considered and audacious, attempt at innovation. This is not designed to encourage failure, rather it is to encourage people to persist after they have experienced setbacks. It's the acknowledgement that even with rational, logical thinking we will not necessarily get it right on the first, second, or even tenth go.

7. **Not being able to embrace ambiguity.** I get it. In the corporate world there is often an expectation we will have all the answers up front, know the numbers for cost and return on investment, the resources required, and the list goes on … This doesn't provide permission or space to explore. Embrace the unknown and be comfortable being uncomfortable to experiment with new and bold ideas.

Cultures, particularly subcultures inside organisations, are particularly fragile. Culture is an effect, not a cause. It's the thing you get and not the lever you pull. With this in mind, you need to consider the 'garbage in, garbage out' context of your innovation program. If you consider this through the lens of the people you are asking to participate in your innovation program and you do not deliver on the promise, you effectively trigger impending doom for your innovation culture.

Sounds dramatic. It's not. I spend hours, days, and often many weeks with employees of all different levels, not only to hear their ideas but to understand their mindset and views of innovation inside their organisation. The above seven killers are the issues that are shared with me time and time again. It's said that a person's perception is their reality, and if the perception your people have is that innovation isn't real then you can see this as the death of your innovation culture.

* * *

But this doesn't have to be all doom and gloom because it can be recoverable.

If you want to avoid an innovation graveyard and the death of your innovation culture, change the system. One of the biggest benefits of implementing the Corporate Innervation Operating System is the uplift in culture. Culture cannot be imported, copied, or borrowed. It is an outcome of your systems and consistent coaching and development of your people to build an innovation culture. The takeaways you can focus on immediately with your people are:

- Reframe your language to one of 'Yes, and … ' to ensure your response does not seem like an immediate criticism – open the conversation to constructive exploration.

- Listen, listen, and then listen some more to all ideas, and follow up with action. Don't let innovation become just another buzzword so that people's eyes start glazing over every time it is mentioned.

- Get really comfortable being uncomfortable, and in the words of the Tata Group, 'Dare to Try'.

- Focus on the opportunities and remove any emotional attachment to ideas to allow a deeper discussion and exploration with people interested in the idea.

- Stamp out internal competition, siloed thinking, and any process that inhibits the sharing of information and cross-pollination of ideas.

PART III

Creating a Corporate Innervation Operating System that adds value to the bottom line

CORPORATE INNERVATION is about much more than just the idea and final product. It is focused on maximising the human element of innovation inside an organisation. To be successful, you need to master the human element because your people are the most important component in your Corporate Innervation Operating System. You can have a structured process and incredible ideas, but without your people to make it work and bring ideas to life you are likely to end up with just another vanilla program of work.

In the corporate environment, innovation is less about luck and more about empowering your people to explore their ideas and bring them to life. There is an art to this, and you need to disentangle the process from the people to ensure you select the right people to guide, mentor, and support the delivery of innovation in your organisation.

As you go through this section and the Corporate Innervation Operating System framework, focus on how you can grow and develop the culture of innovation inside your organisation through considering the following:

- Your **innovation culture** needs to be powerful to attract people inside the organisation to want to participate. This is your brand, and you want it to be strong, powerful, and inclusive. Your brand and culture need to show that you are all in it together.

- Consider **employee engagement**:

  - insist on **communication** that is a two-way dialogue so your people know their ideas will be heard and taken seriously

  - provide **psychological safety** to create the space to discuss any idea, no matter how quirky, different, or boring

  - have a **collaborative approach** to show that everyone has something to contribute to the overall success of the program

- provide **growth and development** opportunities for people through working on collaborative projects that may be different from their 'day job', growing and expanding their skills and network.

• Consider the impact on their **performance and happiness** at work through providing your people with a voice and opinion on how to shape the future of the organisation. Not only does this inspire people to be more productive and positive in the workplace, but it can also help to attract good talent from outside.

8

What makes a great innovation leader?

Ideas and employees are the heroes of your innovation framework, and your innovation leaders are their guides.

Okay, so by now you'll see why innovation is not something that is done in isolation by the chosen few, nor is the innovation manager the guru of all ideas and new technology. We need to get rid of that thinking. In some instances, we'll really need to switch the thinking of how we view the innovation leaders in our organisation. The ideas and employees are the heroes of your innovation framework, and your innovation leaders and teams are the guides that will teach and encourage these people from the genesis of an idea to implementation if successful.

Innovation is a game everyone should be able to play.

Seek out innovation leaders who dare to be different and do the things that others are not willing to do. Find a change agent and risk taker who thrives with a creative environment, healthy conflict, and robust conversations about the ideas that are right for the organisation. These people are born to win, not at all costs, but with integrity, hard work, and dedication to the long-term vision of an innovation culture.

There are seven characteristics that make really successful corporate innovation leaders:

1. Having a deep curiosity for everything that relates to the organisation.

2. Being bold and daring.

3. Having a compelling vision to build a culture people want to be a part of.

4. Coaching people like a team of champions.

5. Being a problem-solver.

6. Being transparent and a driver of continuous open lines of communication.

7. Being a tribe builder.

Let's have a look at each of these.

A DEEP CURIOSITY FOR EVERYTHING THAT RELATES TO THE ORGANISATION

These are the people who are curious about *everything*. You know the ones: they are always asking questions. They want to know about all aspects and machinations of the organisation and industry they work within.

Their inquisitive nature also goes well beyond this because they are open to every idea that comes their way, and they look at it with an open mind. These people are focused on the ideas of the people from within their organisation, not just the ideas they have themselves.

They know they need to look down and into the organisation to find and drag out the genius ideas, not up and towards their leaders for their own benefit.

BOLD AND DARING

You want your innovation leaders to be bold and daring, with a real sense of bravado. This is not someone who is easily intimidated, and they are masters of resisting pressure to return to 'what we've always done'. For the right ideas, they will need to know how to structure a discussion to position these ideas with the leadership team for support. They will need to know how to support ad-hoc innovation ideas in the corporate world of budgeting, strategy, and large programs of work. You need someone who can duck and weave through the system to push up against the blockers and advocate for the right ideas.

Great ideas shouldn't have to wait until the next planning cycle. You need someone who can diplomatically challenge the status quo. Innovation is never on time, and it doesn't fit into budgeting and resource allocation timetables.

A COMPELLING VISION TO BUILD A CULTURE PEOPLE WANT TO BE A PART OF

Your people are the lifeblood of innovation. A great innovation leader humanises the process by putting people at the centre of everything.

Your innovation team and your innovation leaders need to stand for more than the values behind innovation. This is more than just doing something fun and creating new ideas. This is about building the innovation culture of the organisation, and creating the space for people to think differently and explore their ideas. This is about building a space where everyone is equal. This is a safe space. There is psychological safety and people can talk about their ideas without fear of ridicule.

Being optimistic, collaborative, and emotionally intelligent are key attributes you need to look for to build the vision of innovation and establish the culture throughout your organisation. Your innovation leader will not be afraid of failure, rather their fear is in never trying. This needs to be cultivated in their team and throughout the organisation.

COACHING PEOPLE LIKE A TEAM OF CHAMPIONS

This isn't about your innovation team or your innovation leader pursuing their own personal goals and personal ideas. It's also not about bringing in an ex-head of a startup and giving them the remit of putting together an in-house startup. This shouldn't be an artist-in-residence program where your employees observe the work of someone else. This is about guiding and teaching people to get their hands dirty in the innovation process.

Your innovation leader must have a desire to teach, support, and guide their colleagues on the journey of innovation. They are not there to take credit. They're not there to be seen as the hero. As an innovation coach they need to bring out the best in people through seeing their untapped potential.

Like all coaches of great champions, you want your innovation leader to challenge and demand a lot of your employees and how they engage in innovation, to push them to their limits to accelerate their rate of learning and develop their skills to develop and implement winning ideas. As I said earlier, this is not an extracurricular activity that they only tap into for innovation, but rather something they can utilise in all aspects of their work.

The problem with coaching teams is the same problem a coach of a track athlete has. As an audience, we generally only remember the last sprint to the finish line. We don't see the hours of strength training, running drills, and gut-wrenching training that happens for years before a race.

Innovation and organisations are multi-dimensional constructs that require bespoke 'training' schedules to suit the team. This will never be a one-size-fits-all approach. A good innovation leader works with people to develop, enhance, and grow their skills so by the time they get to the last sprint, they are strong, prepared, and fit to deliver.

A PROBLEM SOLVER

Intuition, logic, and the love of seeing a problem as a great thinking challenge will be required to push boundaries. Your innovation leader needs to take your employees through the whole lifecycle of innovation, and all the ups and downs, failures, setbacks, and successes. Solving problems and unblocking processes in the business will be part of their day-to-day, so this person needs to thrive on looking at things from a different perspective, and not get frustrated and flustered. You want someone who can drive hard and really push (diplomatically, of course) and then get back in the ring and do it again the next day.

This is not a brutish, stubborn person who runs roughshod over the people around them to ensure the success of their ideas. Quite the opposite; you want someone with exceptional interpersonal and communication skills to work with all members of the organisation to bring people together, share information, and come up with trusted solutions. Problem-solving is a team sport, and this person needs to be a team player.

TRANSPARENT AND A DRIVER OF CONTINUOUS OPEN LINES OF COMMUNICATION

This is where it can get a little tough. If you want your innovation culture to thrive, you need a leader who operates with a methodology of full disclosure with their teams, profound honesty, and continuous open lines of communication. They really need to walk their talk on this one, because without transparency, little whispers that you can't control will occur over different projects and ideas, and before you know it some backchanneling and politicking will occur to erode an idea.

By building trust, openness, and a culture of inclusivity in all forms of innovation, anxiety will be reduced and collaboration will be easier to achieve. Trust begets trust. This person needs to lead by example and commit to being an open leader, and encourage others to follow their lead.

Transparency and trusting relationships developed throughout the organisation will extend to the innovation projects being worked on. Easy access to information and ideas in development will encourage collaboration and support throughout the lifecycle of an idea. You want to open up the pathways to information and wisdom that otherwise may not have been accessible because it's in the heads of people who work in the organisation.

When trust and transparency are in place and working, your innovation leader has developed a safe space for detractors of an idea to discuss the reasons why they think it may not work. These open, honest, and hard conversations are extremely valuable, and are important to the development and possible success of ideas. We can sometimes learn more from the reasons why people think something won't work than the heady reasons why we love an idea.

Collaboration is more than just happy high fives in a multi-disciplinary team; it's working through barriers, problems, and negative feedback to ensure an idea is robust. And if something isn't going to work, it's better to know this sooner rather than later. In my experience, a detractor who is listened to and really heard can become one of the biggest advocates for your innovation culture because it shows them you're in it to provide value and not just tick boxes and deliver mindless projects.

A TRIBE BUILDER

'Growing a tribe' is a bit of an entrepreneurial buzz term at the moment, but whether you call it your tribe, community, or internal network, it's an integral part of building an innovation culture. This is part of building an inclusive community to support the growth and development of innovation throughout the organisation.

Your innovation leader needs to know and love the tribe that they build. That might sound a bit woo-woo, but it's this community that will grow the new culture and create positive change. It will start small, with a group of self-selecting individuals who either want to learn more about innovation or feel they have a lot to give to the community. It's then about how they nurture and attract people to the tribe until it becomes part of the pulse of the organisation.

This is one of the elements I rarely see inside organisations, and it's not through a lack of trying. The problem is a lack of authenticity.

* * *

You can have any tool, and you can implement any software system to capture ideas, and you can have any way of working in your organisation, but if you don't have these fundamental traits of good innovation leaders, you won't succeed. And you must allow them to guide, coach, and build an inclusive community for your organisation.

Ideas and employees are the heroes of your innovation framework, and your innovation leaders are their guides. It's crucial to have the right people in these roles to develop skills, confidence, and the right attributes in your people. The emotional intelligence and leadership skills of your innovation leaders will drive how people participate in your innovation program.

Your people are the lifeblood of your innovation process

*People are the backbone of your innovation program – if you
don't give them the ability to deliver, they won't.*

I f you don't listen to your people, either they'll stop talking to you
or they'll go somewhere they feel they are being heard. As a leader,
you need to invest time in your people and listen to what they
have to say. You need to lean right into their ideas and visions for
the future. These are the people who walk into work every day to
dedicate their time and headspace to their project, customers, teams,
or whatever area they work in. Through the Corporate Innervation
Operating System, we want to create an innovation culture built on
the principles of an open, communicative, and collaborative culture.
As a leader, you always need to be listening.

There is an ever-increasing expectation among workforces to be
heard, express an opinion, and have stimulating work that will grow
their skills and stretch their thinking. It will not always be easy to
balance the ideas and passions of your people with the day-to-day
requirements of work, but if you don't try they'll find another leader
or organisation that will.

A survey of over 1500 C-Suite Executives in 2019 found that the biggest concern of this cohort wasn't disruption, disruptive technology, or retaining customer loyalty, it was keeping good people.[1] Yep, the knowledge that not only are good people hard to find, they're even harder to hold on to because they are continually seeking experiences and values that align with their expectations. Let's not forget that the gig economy and ease of starting their own business gives people a multitude of options to consider before they commit to a full-time opportunity.

I'm sure by now you know my view on cereal buffets, free pizza, beanbags, and more to cultivate a cool factor, which can be appealing to some but really is more about innovation theatre than the long-term added value to an employee. These 'benefits' will wear thin, and become meaningless over time if there are no new challenges. The opportunity to develop and work on an innovation project will satisfy personal and professional goals for many in your business.

LISTENING TO YOUR PEOPLE

There are four key areas of listening to your people:

1. **Providing psychological safety.** This is a theme that is repeated throughout the book, and for good reason. You want your people to be authentic, happy, and productive. That's not possible if they are operating in an environment where they are afraid to provide new ideas, test something and fail, or be brutally honest without fear of consequences. Innovation cannot occur without a place to be a little different, crazy, and have the trust of the people around you to support you in the process. This is not something that can be solved overnight if you are operating in an environment where there is some degree of distrust or lack of transparency. As a leader, you need to cultivate psychological safety daily. This is not something that can be a set-and-forget process

---

1   C-Suite Challenge 2019.

because you stated your intention. It's something that takes time, daily conversations, and proof over time.

2. **Making yourself available.** It is not enough to be visible. That's a no-brainer in our world of open-plan offices. Provide the time, space, and emotional availability to have conversations about ideas, blockages, or problems. Be open to both the tough and uncomfortable conversations as well as the abstract and conceptual brainstorming ones. By connecting with the people of the organisation to talk about anything and everything, you will strengthen your relationships and the culture of listening in the organisation.

3. **Looking out for the non-verbal cues.** Innovation isn't an exclusive game for extroverted people who take great pleasure in vocalising their ideas and opinions to spark discussions. Look for the introverts, the people who may feel a little shy or unsure about how to share their thoughts and ideas, and carve out the time to talk with them. My experience with innovation in the corporate environment is that less than one-third of ideas come out in open forum meetings. The most productive conversations are often when I run into people at the coffee machine, walking between meetings, when they ask for a quiet chat, or any other circumstance outside the more public meeting environment. Too often the corporate environment can be quite competitive, and people want to be right and seen as an authority when they speak up.

4. **Finding the balance.** A healthy balance between business as usual work and the additional work, time, and emotional energy required for innovation projects can be difficult to find sometimes. Every one of your people is more than their role in the organisation, and we don't want them to feel they are drowning trying to complete an innovation as quickly as possible. Remember, innovation is *not* part of hustle culture, although it is often portrayed this way. Encourage your teams to find a sustainable cadence in their work. Consistency is key.

So, that's the theory – what happens next? This needs to be turned into action. It's important to make the space for the ideas and conversations, but it will be meaningless unless this is followed up with *action*. 'Innovation' is a doing word. Action, meaningful follow-up, and transparency in the process about what is happening with the ideas are critical.

Conversations, suggestions, and ideas that are floated and then disappear can be harmful. Remember, this falls into the category of theatre of innovation as opposed to the implementation and management of an inclusive, productive process. Your people are the lifeblood of your innovation process. Invest in your people, not just with a framework but with your time. Listen to them and make them part of the process, otherwise you'll end up with a culture of people who don't share their ideas.

PART IV

**Building the framework
inside your organisation for
growth and transformation**

TO GET THE MOST out of this section and the Corporate Innervation Operating System, you need to dedicate your focus to the *process* and not the *outcomes*. People, ideas, market externalities, pandemics, you name it – stuff will go wrong from time to time, but when you have a process, people, and culture all focused on diligently making sound decisions to support the organisation, you will have a more robust innovation process that will stand the test of time.

Like a good investor, you have to be comfortable with uncertainty, know how to play the long game, and understand your strengths and weaknesses so you don't get caught in your own outmoded patterns. You will need to be really comfortable getting uncomfortable, because while it sounds easy, it takes a considerable amount of focus, effort, and diligence to establish an innovation process built on sound decision-making and a considered customer focus.

Corporate Innervation is about the people, processes, and longevity of an innovation culture that will last well beyond the tenure of your current leadership and innovation team. It's not about the ideas. They're easy to find. Corporate Innervation is about the development of skills and behaviours to manage and develop the culture of innovation. High-performing teams come into their own when things go south, and with innovation it's never a smooth or easy ride to the finish line. The embedded skills, attributes, and processes will inform how your innovation program will perform.

This is not about chance or luck. It is about heightening the element of skill and objectivity and creating a process of success through the management of uncertainty. Your people can be taught to think in a way that creates a collaborative and innovative culture for growth, rather than the short-term, flashy quick win.

As you go through each step of the Corporate Innervation Operating System, focus on the process and not the outcome of each idea. The purpose of this is to hone your skills on the decision-making process required for each step and to understand that you need to go all-in on this framework. Boots and all.

You are building more than a process, you are building a culture that will become bigger than the innovation portfolio.

Step one: define the light on the hill

This is the moment the leadership team must define innovation and what it means to the business. You set the tone, vision, and mission for your organisation's pursuit of innovation. If you don't have a purpose or goal, you need to question what you are doing. Innovation for innovation's sake will never make sense.

You will require an inspirational mission for innovation, and a compelling narrative that brings everyone together in the organisation to focus on the same targets and future. The mission for innovation is bigger than furthering any professional, divisional, or team self-interests; you're asking the organisation to be a part of something that is bigger than any individual.

You're probably saying to yourself that you already do this with your overall values and strategy, and I'm sure you do. The challenge is that despite the understanding of overall strategy, divisions, teams, and in some instances, leaders can default to a position of self-interest to ensure their personal deliverables and performance targets are achieved. Performance measurement mechanisms have conditioned leaders to compete against their peers, and this is not viable for an innovation process.

You need to send a powerful message that this is about building a strong core of innovation focused on building social capital inside the organisation to unlock human potential and the genius inside the organisation. You are planning for and anticipating the future, and you are building it together.

A lot of time can go into the development of the words, sentences, and pretty diagrams we use to share the vision. Often too much time. Don't overthink it. Align the vision for innovation with the business strategy you have in place. Organisations need to understand that they define what innovation means to them. It cannot be a 'know it when I see it' process; well, not if you want a focused portfolio of innovation that will provide real benefits.

You are doing this to put people at the centre of your plan for innovation, but you need to ensure that everyone is moving in the same direction and focused on the same future outcomes. Your agenda for innovation needs to include:

- knowing the right mountain to climb
- developing future markets for growth
- building an innovation community inside the organisation
- unlocking human potential and developing the skills of your people
- having a self-sustaining innovation process.

Let's have a look at each of these.

CLIMBING THE RIGHT MOUNTAIN

It is obvious that we want everyone to be climbing the right mountain. Unless you make this clear, your innovation process will get off track and before you know it you'll have people pitching for self-driving cars and ideas that sound incredibly fun but are not relevant for your growth targets. Be clear about where you want to go, the rules of engagement, and the boundaries for how far people can go. Do this gently and carefully, because you don't want to temper the enthusiasm of employees with ideas, but you do want them to work within an understanding of what may be attainable. Give them enough guidance so their ideas will make sense to the future vision of the organisation and then let their imaginations run wild.

Okay, this sounds like I am stating the bleeding obvious, and for some I am, but I see this regularly as something that is missing. What I see frequently is an academic definition of innovation coupled with unachievable unicorn examples, such as, 'How do we become the next Uber?' This is more than just unattainable for multi-faceted organisations, it is off-putting. It makes people other than the super-confident reconsider their ideas. Often these ideas will stay in the minds of these people as they fear the ideas are not 'big' enough.

An unattainable mission alienates your people and sets your innovation framework up for the graveyard. Innovation is not a trend, and has been around since the inception of business; large organisations are just really bad at focusing and prioritising innovation in a way that makes sense.

The message from the top down needs to be clear about the direction you are heading and your objectives. You must define the destination, point your people in the right direction, and let them go for it. It will be like herding cats. There will be a range of ideas that vary from benign, simple, incremental changes to radical suggestions that raise a few eyebrows, and everything in between. When your people are thinking about it, they're participating.

The speed at which you climb the mountain is not important. What *is* important is that you are choosing the right mountain to climb. *Effectiveness* will be more important than *efficiency*, and you will need to measure this over time. Don't leave this to chance or a 'feeling'. Continually assess the ideas, portfolio, and outcomes to make sure you are climbing the chosen mountain and heading towards the summit. Mountain climbing, like innovation, is a skill honed and developed over time.

DEVELOPING FUTURE MARKETS FOR GROWTH

You want the entire organisation to participate in the identification of future markets, the creation of new revenue streams, and the realisation of these ideas. For some this will be a tectonic shift: a collective vision as opposed to a handed-down plan. Your biggest resource and your biggest advantage will be the creativity, inventiveness, and problem-solving capability of your people. Grab it and harness their capability to build and develop the biggest asset you have in the organisation. The creation of a strong organisation does not rest solely on the shoulders of the board and executive leadership team.

BUILDING AN INNOVATION COMMUNITY INSIDE THE ORGANISATION

This mission, purpose, and vision needs to be greater than just the dollars on the bottom line. Innovation will help shape the culture and performance of your organisation well into the future. You are investing in your human capital to strengthen the skills, knowledge, and capability of everyone.

Utilise the people who are passionate and keen to grow their innovation skills to build an internal community to support continuous learning, growth, and development. Commit to innovation as a bona fide part of your organisation by supporting the development of champions, mentors, and guides in all areas of your organisation.

Thinking, sharing, and learning together will support the vision of innovation from the bottom up. The pursuit of a common goal by many people, rather than just the leaders, will enhance your ability to make innovation part of the fabric of the enterprise, and not just a separate function.

We often learn more by doing and being immersed in a process in the corporate world. The social process of learning will support the development of an organisation-wide culture, implementation of a way of working, and empowerment to deliver. Your innovation community will integrate knowledge, the tools, and selected delivery methodology throughout the organisation, and support the uplift of skills of all employees.

UNLOCKING HUMAN POTENTIAL

The best innovation ideas do not usually come from the board or executive or management meetings. This is not saying the leadership team has no role to play in innovation, rather it's time to turn to your employees for their ideas. Give everyone permission to be creative and use their ingenuity to solve any problems, gaps, or new market solutions. It's imperative that this is not just lots of noise and no progress. Your people will not continue to support an innovation framework that is just for show.

The genius is in your people. They see the problems, challenges, and opportunities every day. It's time to give them a voice.

A SELF-SUSTAINING INNOVATION MODEL

As you set the tone for innovation in your organisation, you also need to be clear that you should be building a self-sustaining model. This will not be a money pit to play around with ideas as an engagement strategy. While there will be wins and losses, the purpose is to develop a portfolio where the revenue supports the conceptual development of future projects. If you are consistently funding a process that doesn't provide any return on investment to the organisation, your innovation function will quickly fall away through eroded budgets and lack of resources.

An innovation portfolio that requires a permanent sinking fund will eventually find itself closed for business.

* * *

Here are the fundamentals of step one:

- Create an explicitly clear mission, vision, and strategy for innovation to get everyone moving in the right direction. Don't be ambiguous on the goals and vision for the future. Give your people the direction and allow them to creatively help you fill the gaps on how to get there.

- Be inspirational and inclusive. Give everyone permission to support their vision and strategy through the development of their ideas.

- Move forward with clarity and an aligned aspiration for your innovation goals and the long-term strategic direction of the organisation.

- Rethink your process to focus on your people and build an innovation community.

The following steps in the framework take you through the process, purpose, and non-negotiables for embedding an innovation mission in your organisation and focusing everyone on the right mountain to climb.

Step two: align from the top

Your vision, mission, and goals for innovation are clear and you are herding everyone towards the right mountain to climb. The next step requires the swift alignment of all key influencers in the organisation to ensure a consistent message and a clear understanding of the mandate. Embrace innovation as a collective opportunity that benefits the entire organisation, even if that means your team are participating and your division is not receiving a direct tangible benefit. The purpose is to implement a Corporate Innervation Operating System that builds a better future for the organisation.

Leave your ego at the door. This requires humility and emotional intelligence to go through ideas and make it all about the people and customers you are serving. In corporate speak, a lot of terms are thrown around like 'thinking from the outside in', 'design thinking', 'voice of the customer' ... and I could keep going, but what I often see is a form of internal lobbying by leaders to have their project prioritised or resourced over something else in the business for personal benefit rather than the good of the business.

The steps to do this sound easy, and in theory it's relatively straightforward, but like many things, the simple aspects can be hard to implement.

ALIGN KEY LEADERS AND INFLUENCERS EARLY

Bring all the key stakeholders into the conversation early. Drive the message from the top that the board, executive leadership team, other leaders, and internal influencers are all on the same page. You are aiming for unwavering collaboration at all levels of the organisation. This is not just for the strategy; everyone needs to be on board and supporting the process from day one, so it's imperative the conversations and engagement process happen early. All too often I see innovation projects avoid the risk, finance, and people and performance conversations until the last minute, generally through fear of being told 'no' or asked to do it another way – the way they've always done it. Involve all areas of the organisation early and make them advocates and enablers of the process.

Consistent messaging and solidarity from the leadership team to invest in and follow the Corporate Innervation Operating System is required to create momentum from the bottom up. Develop a network of influencers and leaders so strong they'll correct anything that falls off track.

SET UP THE INNOVATION MANDATE

Innovation will require investment in terms of budget, time, resources, and on occasion space to co-locate teams. Charter, mandate, and provide a delegation of authority to manage the selection, resourcing, and funding of the innovation process. The aim is to move from a staccato process broken up through handover and approval requirements to an autonomous innovation system with a smooth end-to-end responsibility for design and delivery. Consolidated and modernised roles reduce delays, minimise overlaps, and simplify accountabilities.

Create an investment committee to determine, validate, and release funds for innovation incubation projects. This committee needs to be representative of all divisions and business units in the organisation. The role of this committee is to align innovation to strategy and manage the framework architecture against long-term initiatives, organisation and divisional plans, and quarterly priorities.

To ensure innovation decisions are not made in a vacuum, the committee will be required to understand the macro, micro, and external economic factors to consider impacts and possible risks throughout the process. Consider all internal programs to stop duplication, inconsistencies, or new projects that will be in conflict with other projects.

Think of this like a mini board inside the organisation to implement the strategic direction of innovation, release funding, and allocate resources to projects. Make it representative of the entire organisation and choose the people with the right skills and attitudes. Ask internal candidates to apply for these roles and put them through an application and interview process, not only to assess their level of genuine interest, but also to elevate the positions in the organisation. You don't want this to devolve into another steering committee or talk fest.

To really make it work, this needs to be an investment committee with a delegated authority to decide, prioritise, and resource innovation projects and be accountable for the success of the innovation portfolio.

AGREE TO A SPECIFIC SET OF METRICS AND GOALS TO DEFINE SUCCESS

Just like your definition of innovation, success will not be a 'know it when you see it' process. Make your definition of success clear, succinct, and measurable. Define the goals and benefits you want to achieve through your Corporate Innervation Operating System and establish metrics to measure them.

Benefits realisation can be a touchy subject, and that's amplified when applying the process to innovation. Despite the good, bad, and ugly of benefits realisation and how it may be applied to your organisation overall, you must ensure you have a process of identifying, planning, managing, and analysing your intended benefits from any investment in innovation. Given the nature of innovation, this should not be the driver of an initial investment decision, but you will need an evolving process to assess the benefits of each project and the overall portfolio.

Benefits realisation is a bit of a can of worms, and there are many ways to do it, and do it well – or poorly. Don't fall into the trap of selecting targets that are too easy to attain so the scorecard looks sensational. We can't expect to get an innovation right first time, and it will be incredibly tempting to adjust figures to accommodate any scope changes, budget changes and the like, but if you want to get better at estimating and understanding your innovation process you need to work with your original baseline and examine and learn from the changes that happen in the course of the project. I see project managers adjusting figures all the time to show a positive outcome, but we don't learn anything through sanitised stories.

A SELF-SUSTAINING INNOVATION PORTFOLIO

Your objective is to create a self-sustaining innovation portfolio so the innovation leaders will not continually be going cap in hand for funding. Let's be frank: innovation will be hamstrung and inconsistent if teams are constantly seeking funds out of the budget cycle. Initially it should be expected that the innovation portfolio will operate on a J-curve or S-curve basis and require funding through the budget allocation process for the first few years. Think of this like you would a new business. It needs to start somewhere with some investment, but will eventually need to pay for itself.

The innovation investment committee will have oversight and management of the funds to deliver innovation. There will always be the exception that is beyond their delegated level of authority or funding capability, and when this occurs the investment committee can provide a business case to the executive leadership team if they feel strongly about the project.

It may seem a bit counterintuitive at first, but it's important to keep all innovation projects together in the one portfolio, even after they have been implemented and start to run as business as usual. To become self-sustaining, you will need to reinvest the benefits into the conceptual development and incubation of new innovation ideas to create a self-funding model. You will need to take the good with the bad. Not all innovations will make money; some will not take off, and others may provide intangible benefits only. A good investment model will manage this and the selection of innovation projects.

Create a mandate, decision process, and prioritisation model that will allow for a balanced and sustainable investment approach. The Corporate Innervation Operating System will have longevity in your organisation because this self-funding model fuels the step change needed in the business process and culture while maintaining momentum.

PUT EVERYTHING ON THE TABLE TACTICALLY

A credible innovation portfolio involves a level of scrutiny over all relevant high-value ideas and projects. An examination of every innovation idea and project from all lines of business needs to be undertaken to understand what you may already have in progress, have planned, or be considering. This is not the time to keep innovation projects out of this process, unless they are at such an advanced stage of delivery that it would not make sense. No lobbying for side projects or the ability to keep the sneaky ones elsewhere in other portfolios.

Now you can create a portfolio and process to manage the innovation portfolio. It can be a project management office with a standardised delivery framework, a reporting and benefits process to coordinate the delivery of these projects, or whatever suits the organisation and reporting requirements. Given the nature and varying levels of maturity of the ideas and projects, this can be a rudimentary and simplified delivery framework focused on the consistency of process, reporting, and delivery outcomes as opposed to mandating a specific project management methodology.

This is the point of no return ...

* * *

For the Corporate Innervation Operating System to work effectively in your organisation you must:

- make the effort to build an innovation portfolio and investment process to manage ideas and projects and support the development of a truly connected and supported innovation ecosystem inside your organisation

- be clear your objective is to monetise the whole ecosystem and not just one project at a time

- understand that no matter how much planning, research, and time are put into innovation projects, there will always be some that just fail to engage the market, so give yourself the edge by building an entire portfolio and not just one project.

Step three: give your employees a voice

The third, and really critical part, of putting together the Corporate Innervation Operating System is to giving your employees a voice. You can put the best tools and processes in place, have the most incredible communication with your employees, but unless you have a mechanism to tap into their genius, your innovation process will not be as powerful as you would like it to be. They have all the gold inside their heads. You just need to learn how to tap into it and give them the opportunity to tell you what you need to know.

In my experience this can be the part that makes or breaks corporate innovation. Why? If only lip service is paid to ideas and they fall into a black hole and are never heard of again, you can guarantee you will erode any confidence or belief in the system and people will be extremely unlikely to continue to provide their ideas. This doesn't mean you need to action every idea immediately. Not only will you not have the time and resources to manage that, but not every idea will be relevant, timely, or meet the overarching goals of the organisation. But all ideas will need to be considered and treated with respect.

Remember, trust begets trust. Your people are trusting you with their ideas. Show them the respect they deserve.

THE BEST IDEAS ARE SUBMITTED WHEN YOU LEAST EXPECT IT

One of the best things to do is provide them with a mechanism they can access any time no matter where they are. One of the things I have found to be the most successful is having an online process employees can access on their computer or through an app. With all the companies I've worked with, the best ideas are submitted when you least expect it.

A technology solution will be integral to the success of this step. We want people to feel the freedom to think about their ideas when it suits. A technology solution, preferably one that supports an app on a smartphone, allows people to submit their ideas whenever their brain explosions happen.

This is stuff you can't plan for. I love it when I get emails and notifications for new ideas that have been submitted on the weekend or late at night. Or the ones that come in at two o'clock in the morning after a few drinks and they send me an email saying, 'I have this great idea'. It always makes me smile and I have a bit of excitement about the idea. These are the real ideas drawn on a napkin, and you can bet there's a bit of bravado after a few drinks. If they've been dwelling on it for a while they can be a bit sheepish in the initial conversation, but they're relieved they are finally actioning their idea. People have even sat on ideas for years before they've felt comfortable putting them forward.

This also provides what I call the 'virtual bedside notebook'. You know that thought that either wakes you up in the middle of the night or stops you from sleeping? If this is an innovation idea, I encourage people to submit it directly into the app. Don't write it down to be shoved into a drawer or lost in a notebook. Don't worry if it's unstructured, unformed, or just some really high-level thinking. Sending the idea through gives the innovation team an opportunity to work through the idea with the person and assess if there is something in it for the organisation. An idea they otherwise may not have received. And hopefully this gives the employee back some much needed sleep.

Your employees know your internal and external customers, processes, and business inside and out. They know your internal and external pain points intimately. And they often have the best and most functional ideas to solve these pain points. So, make it easy for them to tell you.

This is a challenge in more than just corporate innovation: if employees don't have a channel for their ideas to be taken seriously, they will not share them with you. Trust me, these are the ideas that actually can make a significant difference to the organisation. There's no innovate-on-demand here. They aren't the spur-of-the-moment brainstorming ideas; they've been dwelling on them, keeping themselves up at night wondering how to implement them, and we need to give them a platform to share and develop these ideas. It needs to be open, transparent, and really, really easy.

WHAT IT *DOESN'T* LOOK LIKE

Hackathons and competitions

This is a really controversial point of view, so take a few deep breaths and we'll get through this together. 'Hackathons' are no way to give your employees a voice. A hackathon is a competitive piece of theatre where an organisation is seeking innovation from self-selected collaborative teams to come up with their own ideas, create an awesome pitch, and compete for the popularity vote. Great for the extraverts and show ponies, but no way to find the real genius hidden inside your organisation.

I know hackathons are trendy and organisations and management teams love to put them on, but let's get real about them and see them for what they are inside an organisation: theatre. This is not *Shark Tank*.

It seems like it might be fun, but here's where it goes wrong. Even when the hackathon is focused and driving towards a specific outcome or the solution to a problem, they're just leaving it open for the employees to think about whatever they choose to pitch. I know they're trying to gain employee engagement in a really interesting way, but in my experience it doesn't provide the outcomes or engagement that is hoped for.

Here's an interesting scenario that has played out many, many times in many different organisations. A hackathon is put together, with voluntary participation, and different people from across the organisation will join together, form a team, and come up with an idea. Inevitably they will do a ton of work in a very small period of time, pouring their blood, sweat, and tears into it. They will be creating top-line business cases, and looking at financials to see if this can work, and identifying customer segments to see where they believe these ideas can go, and building marketing strategies, market entry points, and go-to-market strategies.

The moment of truth arrives, and the teams take their place to pitch to the audience. What tends to happen here is some really cool, exciting, and playful ideas are pitched and the teams and the audience have some fun. When an excellent pitch is delivered and it's engaging, it grabs the audience – and the value of the idea and how it may or may not fit with the organisational strategy is forgotten. It becomes a popularity and talent contest.

If these ideas are not going to drive revenues or be on the right path for where the organisation is going, it's unlikely anything will happen with them. The problem is that when people participate in these events, they want to see results, and they want to see their solution implemented.

I worked with one organisation where some employees continually mentioned a fabulous idea that won a hackathon, years before I was engaged to work with the organisation. The idea and pitch were sensational. It just wasn't right for the organisation. It was something that had a market, and was likely to do really well revenue wise. But it would have been a very significant transformation to the core of the business and therefore was not within the risk appetite or strategy. It was something the organisation was possibly never going to be ready for. Interestingly, employees were still referring back to it and saw it as management not taking them seriously. And this was years after the event.

And be warned: this effect runs a lot deeper than just how they view innovation. It spreads into trust and a broader feeling of disengagement on how management sees them. They stop believing in you and the culture, and they don't trust in the process. It's very damaging. This disengagement can lead to people leaving the organisation. If this happens, you've lost the brainpower and knowledge that goes along with these people – and that's *not* what we're looking for from a hackathon.

Innovation should not be a popularity contest. It shouldn't be voted on according to how fun it is, or how loudly the audience cheers. What we really need to look at is how good the idea is. By employing a popularity process or voting process and a pitch process like that, we can miss what some people think of as boring ideas. The ideas that aren't sexy. And that is where we miss out on the gold.

We miss out on the Michaels who are giving us the new airport runway light cleaning process. We miss out on the Brevilles that are providing the finger loops on the electric plugs. We miss out on the things that may not be sexy but probably are game changers from a revenue perspective.

Innovation as a standing agenda item in team meetings

It can be a real challenge to provide a platform for ideas, and I often see great intentions getting in the way of providing an open tool for employees. One of the common mistakes I see in organisations is that they do want to give their employees a voice but they're just not sure how to do it. So they turn to idea boxes, brainstorming sessions, and well-meaning leaders and managers setting aside time in their weekly team meetings or monthly catch-ups to come up with innovation ideas.

The problem with this is twofold:

- **Employees really struggle with having to innovate on demand.** They are under pressure to complete a never-ending list of work, provide meaningful updates to their team, and get the help and support required from their leaders and colleagues. Then they are sitting with their peers and feel the pressure to come up with an amazing idea on the spot. They may be shy, or uncertain about how to talk about an unstructured and conceptual idea.

- **What if they have an idea that doesn't directly relate to the team, group, or division they work in?** These ideas are often lost because that team's leader may not be able to relate or see the value in the idea. And in some instances, they don't want to provide a leg up to another manager. No matter the reason, those ideas can be lost completely because they're misunderstood, not in the right area, and may not get the right attention.

MANAGING AND UNDERSTANDING THE IDEAS

Don't underestimate how protective some people will be about their ideas. We really need to honour this in a way that makes sense for the organisation, and also recognises this is the genesis of the idea and it really is only the start of the journey. It's not a done deal at this point.

Often employees will be really protective and emotionally attached to their idea. Not always, but often. They've often been thinking about it for a while. They need some support, tools, and processes to drill into the idea and see if there is something there.

The role of the innovation manager or team at this stage is to work with the person who has submitted the idea and take them through a structured process to flesh out the idea. This is not the time to be the judge and jury on the idea, rather each idea needs to go through a coaching process. It's time consuming, but each idea needs to be assessed on its merits to see how it stacks up in a portfolio of ideas. Don't dismiss the importance of this. Some people won't require this help. The ones that do, you are coaching, guiding, and upskilling.

So how do we do this? I teach innovation teams to move through the following steps.

1. Have strategic conversations

This is quite a disciplined process so that we don't get dragged into the emotion or fun of a new idea. This is structured conversation with the person who has submitted the idea to understand how this idea connects to the narrative of the organisation. Or is it just an innovative idea that doesn't quite fit today? Or ever?

It's a process to discuss the idea in the context of the bigger picture goals and strategic direction of the team, division, or organisation. The purpose is to work through the idea to obtain a deeper understanding and explore if it may have a purpose, solve a problem, support the strategy, or create a revenue stream. Sit down with the employee who has provided the idea, and go through the idea with an open mind to gather information. This should be treated like a discovery – gather as much information as possible. We can be too quick to make decisions on ideas; through this approach I am asking teams to be impartial and gather information only, without a view to making any decisions yet.

2. Standardise the information

Ideas come in all shapes and sizes. I've had ideas that have come through that have been so well researched, accompanied with a structured business case and financial model because they have spent so much time thinking about it. And I have seen others that are merely a paragraph stating the problem and proposed solution. Both of these can be equally valuable or irrelevant, but we need to do the work to make the assessment.

To provide consistency over the thinking and help compare the viability of ideas, I teach teams to structure the information into an 'innovation canvas'.

The purpose of this is to work out at a really high level some answers for the following:

- What is the problem we are trying to solve?
- What are the points of difference for this?
- Will this create an unfair advantage?

- Who are the internal or external customers that will use this solution?

- Do we have the ability to create this solution in-house?

- Do we have any idea of some high-level costs?

- How will we measure any success?

- What are the known risks?

Use this information to understand the business problem, and to dig a little deeper into the potential customer to assess if it will fit into the strategy. Don't over-complicate it. Keep it simple.

3. Create a portfolio of ideas

Once you have done the work on the ideas and have standardised the information, we can start comparing apples with apples and prioritising ideas. Remember, we're not working in a startup environment here. We're working in a structured corporate environment with a detailed long-term strategy, dedicated programs of work, and only minimal headspace for tangential changes. We can be passionate and effusive about an incredible idea, but you and I know that unless it stacks up in a corporate process there will not be any money or resources released to develop an idea. We need money to play, and we need to play the corporate game. Just with minimal viable bureaucracy.

The advantage to having a portfolio of ideas where the information has been somewhat standardised is that you have a funnel of go-to ideas. You will not be able to do everything at once. But having choice is an incredible thing. You can then balance the ideas with the capability, capacity, and urgency of the organisation. The best part ... you will no longer be scrambling for good ideas.

4. It's more than an idea-capturing mechanism

Your people know what's happening inside your organisation. They know how to put these ideas together. They have a view of what they want the future to look like. If you've articulated your strategy correctly, they will show you what's going to make a difference. When this is done right, you don't just tell them what you want the culture to look like, you are allowing them to help shape the culture of innovation and growth in the organisation. You will be taking them on the journey through strategy and delivery to the future horizons of what you envision the company will look like through engaging in their ideas.

* * *

Here are the fundamentals of step three:

- Provide a process and platform for your employees to submit their ideas. Have a mechanism to support the understanding and possible development of these ideas.

- Don't let these ideas fall into a black hole. Follow up each and every one of them and give them the respect and time they deserve.

- Encourage the process and allow employees to think and ponder on ideas.

- Avoid the 'innovate-on-demand' concept in team meetings and other processes.

- Review, assess, and standardise the information provided to allow a decision and prioritisation process to occur.

Step four: walk in your customer's shoes

This is one of my absolute favourite sections of the Corporate Innervation Operating System. This is where the magic happens, the amazing brain explosions, and the joining of the qualitative and quantitative thinking … which my inner nerd really loves.

Ideas, concepts, and strategy can all look fantastic on paper, but we have to recognise that it is too easy for us to get it wrong. Research, particularly market and customer research, is the first hurdle people with a new idea are asked to jump through.

The problem with such research is that humans are terrible forecasters, and they are inclined to tell us what they think their behaviour *would be*, rather than what they actually *do in real life*. Don't just take my word for it; this is an issue that arises frequently for companies that have huge budgets to throw at customer and market research. Coke spent millions market researching a new flavour of Coke to an outstanding and overwhelmingly positive response, but when it was released into the market there was a huge revolt against this product and it turned out to be a huge loss for Coke, financially and in brand equity.

Relying on the voice of the customer and research can be dangerous and has toppled companies in the past. Shoes of Prey was a classic case where the difference between the actual behaviour and intended behaviour was so markedly different, and despite the company diligently following the responses of their customers, it toppled the company. Why? When you ask people about their future behaviour, they answer from their 'system two brain' which is deliberate, fact-loving and logical thinking. As a result market research responders often place a psychological space between their response, which is often a little too optimistic about the likelihood of their future-self behaviour.

When customers move into the buying process, their decisions are usually using the 'system one brain', which is emotional, unconscious, and fast. What happens is the visceral, gut response to either wanting something or not. At this point the customer, or user, has completely forgotten about the response they gave in the research, and they have moved into a place of comfort, defaulting to their standard response. It is understanding this concept and the users of your product at a much deeper level that will provide insights a survey cannot.[2]

---

2   In the book *Thinking, Fast and Slow*, Daniel Kahneman describes the two different ways the brain forms thoughts and makes decisions, and this has huge implications for how we design and use market research. I highly recommend this book if you are interested in the behavioural science and cognitive biases in our thinking and decision-making.

After the demise of Shoes of Prey, CEO Michael Fox identified the chasm between what the customer says they are going to do, and their actual behaviour saying 'while our mass market customer told us they wanted to customise … what they were consciously telling us and what they subconsciously wanted … were effectively polar opposites.' And, 'despite all the right trends towards personalisation and our success within the customisation niche, contrary to our market research the mass market fashion customer just didn't respond as we expected.'

The hard reality for Shoes of Prey was that consumers thought they wanted to customise their own shoes, and a few people like me did. There's a small, boutique, niche market for these types of unique products. Mainstream customers chose not to take on the risk, expense and uncertainty of customising their own shoes, because the market is already saturated with already designed, on trend, affordable ones. Attempting to scale a small niche product with massive overheads to the mass market broke their business model. Michael Fox stated in retrospect, 'If we'd been able to understand that the mass market customer didn't want to customize, we wouldn't have gone down the path of raising venture capital and instead focused on building a strong but smaller business serving our niche of women who wanted to customize, as we did for the first 2.5 years of the business.'

So how do you truly understand your customer? We can make research tell any story we like. It's too easy to be unconsciously biased, particularly when market research costs eat into your budget and you want to show a result. Always remember it's better to get a real answer rather than one that just looks good on paper.

You need a multi-faceted approach where you only use assumptions to build hypotheses and do not manipulate the outcome of the research. Firstly, you need to ensure that your research isn't a waste of time. Market research should only be the starting point for the creation of hypotheses and profiles, not the final conclusion. Always critically interrogate the results of market research. It's impossible to understand the hard-wired biases of people and their governing internal belief systems from one-dimensional surveys.

Secondly, you need to utilise behavioural economics and observation experimentation methodologies. You must take the time to observe, participate, and get a feel for the process, psychology, and any other factors that determine how your 'subjects' make decisions or operate in that environment.

While I am not suggesting you create a thesis to complete this stage, there is a delicate balance you need to strike between understanding your customer and any assumptions that could lead you astray. I am saying that you need to critically assess all information and utilise your powers of observation to look at all possible outcomes. It cannot be a desk research assignment. One-dimensional information creates one-dimensional results.

TO CHANGE THE WAY YOU THINK, CHANGE THE WAY YOU SEE

The purpose of this step is so much more than research. You are gaining insights and the ability to think beyond your assumptions. Opportunities that you may otherwise have missed can be lurking in the shadows as you are observing and assessing.

Use this step to gain buy-in, create demand, and build advocates for the idea. Give the idea life and soul by showing people what it really means, how it is intended to work, and how value will be measured, either tangibly or intangibly.

This logic can also apply to leaders and executive teams that may not 'get it' when an idea is pitched, or perhaps they don't see the value in the idea. This is an opportunity to move beyond the numbers and ask them to participate or observe the new idea and problem being solved.

The curse of knowledge

If you are a member of an executive team or a leader in an organisation, make it your business to take the time to get teams to walk you through their ideas. Not just in a meeting room, but in situ with the new idea, whether that is in the field or with the potential new user of the system. This is not about the warm and fuzzy aspect of getting out of the office and spending time with your people. I do recommend you do that daily, but there's some legitimate science that sits behind this. Our cognitive biases, often referred to as 'the curse of knowledge' by organisational psychologists, mean that when we know something it's often extremely difficult, and in some cases impossible, to *not* know it. This is why when we are confident in our knowledge about our business and teams we feel we know an answer even if we haven't seen the problem for ourselves.

The problem we need to remove is our propensity to say no to an innovation idea before we truly understand it. This is critical because the same problem occurs when your team discusses ideas with you. Their cognitive bias is now set on the new idea, meaning their new knowledge seems so obvious to them that they may have an unconscious mindset that everyone else knows it too. This can create a disconnection in the translation of an idea at the management table, where jargon, abstractions, and limited explanations may be used to try to convey the idea, as opposed to concrete terms that get everyone on board. See, feel, smell, and touch the idea so you can support it and your team.

This truly is one of the best parts of how to put an innovation idea together. Make it come to life – allow it to be more than a business plan and numbers on a page. You can take an idea from good to great when you can feel yourself in it.

When we work closely on an idea we can easily get to the point we almost can't see it anymore. It becomes difficult to be objective about the idea and the formation of the concept, and at this point it can become too easy to miss the tweaks that will make it go from good to great. I hear it all the time from people that 'they'll pick that up in testing', or, 'we have an iterative process and we'll adjust as we go'. Sounds good in theory, but this fails to achieve the desired results when a team locks onto a concept and iterations are only about the build.

The customer and end user needs are to be considered from start to finish for each idea. This is something the movie industry excels at.

Feedback on concepts, screenplays, and ideas are often collaboratively worked through to elevate and lift an idea to a place they may not have been able to do in isolation.

The movie *Pretty Woman* is a great illustration of how to take something good and make it better by getting into the psyche of the audience. The original screenplay was a lot grittier, and was not the rags-to-riches story that we know and love today. The title of the movie was *3000*, based on the amount of money required to hire a prostitute for a week in LA, and it was originally intended to be a dark drama about sex workers. Audiences hated this concept, and the screenplay was softened to create a romantic feel-good movie, and the director shot multiple different endings. The ending we see today is the one that had an overwhelmingly positive response from the test audiences. I think they nailed it.

There are countless more movie success stories that are almost identical to this: continuous feedback and working directly with the target audience and watching their reactions, not relying on them to share their thoughts. Writers and directors know they are in the business of entertainment, so they work with their peers and audience at every step to try to maximise the success of their movie. Obviously, they don't get this right all the time. Test audiences and shooting multiple endings is expensive. But we don't always need to be extravagant and spend lots of money on this stage. The lesson is about learning to constantly seek feedback, be critical about the information provided, and look for the gaps between actual behaviour and intended behaviour.

Why do they seem to get this better than any one else? They have an intuitive understanding that getting this right can potentially create a new level of demand for the final product. The movie industry is an exceptional example of the intersection of commerce and creativity, and while they don't always get it right, the large studios have obliterated the thinking of build it and they will come.

Think about it? We often know about a potential movie before the screenplay has been written. Why? Feedback from the market drives not only a demand and connection with the project, but becomes a consistent source of test market.

It is almost too easy to become emotionally attached and enamoured by all the things we want to achieve, and the challenge with an innovation idea is we can overdo it in our minds. We can be overenthusiastic, overthink it, and before you know it you have your blinkers on and you're blocking out any external information. We have all been guilty of this. We all get caught up in our own ideas – the challenge is we may not be making an idea that suits the market.

BUT IT LOOKED GREAT ON PAPER ...

This way of thinking and step in the framework is also a critical component in the monetisation step. I work through a nine-step process to support the monetisation of an idea. Like all things, garbage in equals garbage out, so don't gloss over this step and think it's a bit of woo-woo you don't have time for. You'll need all the smarts, information, and objectivity that you've gathered in this step to be able to maximise your monetisation strategy.

We've all learnt through a process of thinking an idea looked stellar on paper but when it came to the wider market it didn't really translate. There is a real gap between the bright, shiny, sexy ideas that the customer doesn't know they want or need yet and getting wider market acceptance. It's important to understand the difference between where we educate our customer and where our customer educates us.

By walking in their shoes, we are asking them to educate us. Remember Michael, the airport runway light cleaner? It wasn't until we went out on the runway with the actual cleaners to see what they were doing that the true depth of the problem, inefficiencies, and safety challenges were understood. It's in these moments we can really start to comprehend what it would mean to create, build, and implement a solution. What was originally thought of as a 'maintenance problem' which could only ever be an expense was completely turned on its head to become an innovation idea. On paper this didn't stack up initially, because we only had qualitative evidence, but by being part of the process and seeing how they work, it became apparent that it needed to be a priority. So we did what all great innovators do; we built a scaled-down prototype to test. Low cost, minimal risk, and maximum engagement from the team doing the light cleaning.

To understand if something is compelling, we need to find out how loudly the drum really beats for this idea. Will it clean the runway airport lights *better*, knowing that we need to exceed the current standard and process and not just meet it? Will the staff get behind it? In this instance it was unbelievably successful, even beyond the expectations of the team putting it together. This became another genius idea hidden in the organisation that was uncovered. Not only did it create efficiencies through being able to work faster, they were able to use fewer staff, significantly less water, and they had cleaner runway lights. They also had an additional benefit that is difficult to put a price on: happy and engaged staff who were seen as contributing to the growth of the organisation.

When we don't understand what our employees are telling us, it may be because we haven't quite got enough information. Maybe we thought it was too simple. Maybe it was overlooked, and, in some instances, it was thought this should be something that is dealt with by their leader or their manager. And maybe there are reasons why that hasn't happened. We need to ensure our own cognitive biases are not getting in the way of having an open mind to a potential new innovation idea. In my experience, the best ideas don't come from the management table or the strategy team. The best ideas come from the least expected people and places in the organisation because they're used to solving their own problems and creating their own workarounds because often it's easier that way.

Don't miss the genius idea inside your organisation because it may not initially look good on paper. Get out and walk in their shoes. Sometimes the small innovations, the unsexy ideas, the ones that we didn't think would be the game changers are the ones that really add value and put the organisation in great stead for a long-term healthy future.

* * *

Here are the fundamentals of step four:

- You need to rethink how you listen to your employees' ideas because it is their insight, knowledge, and deep understanding of how the business works that will give you the genius ideas that you can't see at the board, executive, and leadership tables.

- Try not to solve the ideas from our own understanding of the world. Consider the actual, not stated, behaviour of the customer for each step of the process.

- Remove cognitive bias from your thinking in your assessment of ideas by using a multi-faceted approach to understand the information and data, with a heavy skew on walking in the shoes of the customer.

- As a leader, spend time with both the users and innovation teams to change how you view and understand the project. Numbers and words on paper are very one dimensional; give the idea colour, life, a face, and a personality so you can advocate for it.

Step five: empower your teams to deliver

There's never a shortage of ideas, and rarely is there a shortage of people who, in theory, want to participate in an innovation project. These volunteers are intrinsically motivated and inspired to deliver outcomes that will contribute to the success and growth of the organisation. At this point in the framework you have established a portfolio of ideas, so now you need to step back and let the teams work their magic and shine.

I see a lot of organisations create innovation programs that have no budget and no mandate to deliver. The people in your organisation will see this for what it is: lip service to an idea, with no intention to deliver. If you do this, you will have to make room for an innovation graveyard.

Successful innovation teams are those that have been set up to win through being given a sense of ownership of their role and the autonomy to act on their own accord. If you don't create the opportunity and space for your innovation teams to think, decide, and engage then you are effectively cutting them off at the knees. Empowerment doesn't mean there's no place for the leadership team. Quite the opposite; as leaders you have an integral role to play in supporting the delivery of the final outcome, and this will become clear throughout this section.

The processes, governance structure, and management styles will vary between organisations, but what doesn't change is how good leaders create, guide, and coach empowered teams. Following are my rules for how I coach my clients and leaders to empower innovation teams for success. The purpose and impact of this is more than just getting to the end result, it really is to create a way of working that promotes:

- smart and simple processes
- the fostering of talent and capability
- a culture of innovation and change
- an innovation community
- alignment between the customer, innovation, and strategy to build a logical portfolio for growth.

How are you going to do this?

MINIMUM VIABLE BUREAUCRACY

I know, I know ... the word 'bureaucracy' probably got your hackles up, either with that cold knowing shiver or in complete disgust at the thought of your organisation being referred to as a *bureaucracy*. But let's face it, the way your organisation is run *is* a bureaucracy, and it is that way because it's a complex, multi-faceted system that requires rigid controls and processes. While the word 'bureaucracy' feels like a criticism, organisations need these formal systems to maintain control and ensure long-term survival. You can't have a mobocracy and expect shareholders to be happy.

'Minimum viable bureaucracy' seems like an oxymoron, but what we are aiming for is the balance point between governance, risk, and control and a free-flowing approach that will allow innovation teams to work efficiently, consistently, and creatively. Innovation – taking an idea from a thought bubble into a product or service ready to be implemented – is not a linear process. We need this to be understood to be able to work in a manner that allows teams to add value to the organisation without getting stuck in the quagmire of governance, process, and approval loops.

The challenge for organisations is how they overcome their innate ability to over-engineer a process and create considerable and unnecessary hurdles to be able to be nimble and fast. Your employees only have a certain number of working hours each week, and only a small portion of this may be allocated to an innovation project. If you then weigh them down with too much bureaucracy and red tape, it becomes very hard for them to effectively move forward. They need to spend their time working on the project, not reporting on the project or admin tasks.

What does this really mean? Having just enough structure, processes, tools, and support mechanisms to work in the context of the organisation, but ensuring that it doesn't get in the way of creativity and the team's ability to move through concepts and iterations in an efficient and fast manner. The focus is on developing a flexible and malleable approach to support the overall success of the teams and overall innovation portfolio.

You want your innovation teams to lean right in to the process, test the boundaries, and work in a way that allows them a fast and efficient cadence. As a leader your role is to coach, guide, and mentor them through this process to help the team stay on track, and if any course correction is required you are there to help steer them through the process.

You must understand the following about a minimum viable bureaucracy:

- It is not a free-for-all to create an undocumented project.

- It is not a reduction in your current risk tolerances and processes.

- It is not the ability to work in secret.

- It is not the removal of accountability.

- It is not a report-free zone.

- It is not an undisciplined approach.

The easiest way to do this is to provide a framework. Having *zero* structure is likely to lead to chaos, and it may leave the leaders feeling disempowered, causing them to jump back into either a micro-management mode or a preference not to participate in innovation. If you don't provide some guidance on the boundaries and expectations, you will be setting your teams up to fail. Remember, this needs to be a balance of just enough to maintain focus on the work and supporting documentation, and not being bogged down in the administration of reporting and meetings.

VISION, PURPOSE, AND GOALS

As you would with any major strategy, program, or project, one of the first steps is to align the vision and establish the vision and purpose, and ensure this is in line with the strategy and purpose of the organisation. While it may only be a concept or a thought bubble in the beginning, the team needs to have an understanding of how this may fit into the bigger picture or roadmap of the organisation.

This is an activity that should be run as a workshop with the team, relevant leader, and/or executive sponsor to create a shared vision, purpose, and goals the team are all working towards. It's integral at this point to ensure the vision of the leaders and executives is understood by the team to avoid the possibility of misalignment on completion of the project. This shared vision and purpose can be altered along the way if required, and this can be relatively simple to do from a place of shared understanding.

The focus of all innovation teams needs to be on the outcomes of turning ideas into concepts, and where relevant into an actual product or service to be implemented. The teams will be working iteratively and continually, ensuring they're prioritising the work to fulfil the higher vision and purpose of this innovation.

We need to be intentional to focus on the outcomes and not the tasks. The work defined in each iteration will inform the tasks to be delivered, and this should be self-managed by the team.

GIVE THEM THE RIGHT TOOLS

Provide your innovation teams with a set of tools which can be used as a self-service 'follow the bouncing ball'–style process. Remember, you will be building cross-collaborative teams, and some of these people may not have done this style of work before. We don't need it to be rocket science or involve complex reporting, rather we want to provide the thinking tools, templates, and reporting process to support the team.

Make sure these tools are available to everyone in the organisation. Make this a self-service mechanism that everyone can learn and grow with. As I mentioned earlier, you want the uplift of skills and the building of a community of practice to be a by-product and outcome of a corporate innovation ecosystem, so don't hide the tools away for the use of innovation teams only. I encourage all my clients to ensure their innovation teams take this way of working back into their business-as-usual or regular team environment.

When innovation teams go back to their 'day jobs' (as I find they often refer to their usual tasks), they will take these frameworks, tools, and learnings back to their teams. If they have adapted these tools and methodologies to work more efficiently and effectively, an uplift in skills and an increase in cadence can occur across the board, not just in their innovation teams.

BE CLEAR ABOUT HOW DECISIONS WILL BE MADE

The fundamental idea of empowerment is about allowing the team to make decisions to allow them to continuously move towards the defined goals and objectives. But if you disempower teams by micro-managing and overseeing every task, and wanting to be included in every email or meeting, I can guarantee you will strangle the project by stopping their momentum and ensuring they are completely demotivated. This is leadership 101 stuff, but I continue to see it. If this is you, it really needs to stop because you will never develop the skills, confidence, or culture of your teams.

Again, this is not a free-for-all for the team to make any and all decisions, rather there needs to be a clear understanding of what level of control they have from a decision-making perspective, and what areas they will need to seek guidance or approval on. The control freak in all of us needs to trust our teams to be committed to providing the best possible outcomes for the organisation.

Your role here continues to be coach, guide, and mentor to support them through any grey areas. By being available and supportive, you will continually be involved in the process with the team.

DEFINE THE NON-NEGOTIABLES

Ensure the team is clear on the scope, boundaries, and any risk tolerances so they know the limits on how far they can go. This is not an area that can be a little bit grey and murky. Leave nothing to chance, and then let the team be free to explore, research, test, and measure within the boundaries you have created.

Once your team is clear on the boundaries and non-negotiables, it empowers them to move within those boundaries to test ideas, concepts, and possible solutions. This helps to provide clarity and focus, and aids in removing the bright shiny objects which can distract teams with unimportant tasks or misalignment with the defined vision and goals. Freedom in this way will support free thinking, giving the team an opportunity to develop ideas and concepts that may not have been in their original frame of reference.

Providing boundaries will also give the teams something to push up against. Human nature shows that when the rule breaker, creative thinker, and rebel inside of us all is told that we can't go somewhere, it's likely that we'll test this limit. Listen, coach, and mentor the team through this process. If it is a solution worth investigating then they will have their leader to support them early, rather than surprising them later on. If it's unlikely to be viable or sustainable, this is your opportunity as the leader to gently course correct the team back into an avenue for a viable solution.

ESTABLISH EFFECTIVE COMMUNICATION AND REPORTING

Provide the mechanisms and guidance for the communication and reporting process that you expect from the team. Be clear and leave nothing to chance about how you want them to be accountable. Help the team establish a rhythm for accountability, meetings, and reporting, and allow them to stick with it of their own accord.

Innovation doesn't occur by chance. It requires a process and open feedback loops. Smart, open, and effective communication, not the standard type of reporting that makes everyone look good, on time, and on budget – but doesn't actually achieve anything. For innovation we need to throw that thinking out the window. Innovation requires a deep, gritty honesty, where everyone needs to get comfortable being uncomfortable with the good, the bad, and the sometimes ugly truth about what is happening with a project.

In the bubble of the team there is the safety and security to have the 'oh crap' moments and conversations, and then scramble together to ensure that knowledge stays safely ensconced in the team. This process of saving face and showing the world that everything is hunky-dory needs to be thrown away, never to resurface. We build incredible teams and buy-in through the simple process of no-nonsense communication. Because really, you're only lying to yourself when you are not prepared to own and articulate an accurate representation of your innovation project.

Vulnerability is a strength in effective, open communication. Even when it is tough. When we can embrace brutal honesty and accountability, and be completely transparent on the wins, losses, and failures as a project is in development, we can open ourselves up to solutions to help us succeed. As leaders, innovators, and professionals we will gain more respect, support, and traction with effective communication that's open, frank, and seeks feedback for growth and success.

ESTABLISH AUTONOMY AND AUTHORITY TO DELIVER

Innovation teams are significantly more likely to succeed if you provide them with the autonomy and a delegated level of authority to deliver. And deliver fast. I hear a lot of talk about this, but I don't see enough leaders truly empowering their teams. The word 'empowerment' gets thrown around a lot in leadership circles – most leaders I speak to want to empower their teams. The challenge is it also throws up a lot of fear in leaders that they can lose control or become superfluous, and it is this fear, either conscious or subconscious, that stops them from truly empowering their teams.

For a sustainable and regulated cadence, your team needs the autonomy and authority to deliver. If they are required to consistently stop, seek approval, and manage external expectations, they will spend more time stagnant than they will progressing. The role of the leader is to provide the boundaries, autonomy, and authority to deliver to allow them to be dynamic and get on with the job. With the leader managing the external requirements you can keep the team focused, informed, and empowered.

The greatest challenges are solved by empowered teams. Not by one person. This doesn't come easy to most leaders, and your role here is to develop teams that hold each other accountable. When you have built a team that holds each other accountable, and doesn't let other people wait for their part of the job, you know you have successfully developed a high-performing group.

BECOME PART OF THEIR COACHING AND SUPPORT SQUAD

As a leader in innovation, the role is to enable employees to perform and deliver with the least amount of hindrance possible. This includes the removal of traditional leadership models of command and control, and delegating authority into the team. Your role as a leader changes from exercising power to helping employees unlock their genius and lift their performance and engagement.

It's incredibly important that you are present throughout the entire process. To get the most out of the team your role needs to focus on:

- being a mentor and guide
- being there to course correct, if required
- deflecting external problems to ensure the team isn't distracted with unnecessary tasks or issues
- advocating and championing the project throughout the organisation
- supporting the move through challenges and blockages in the project.

Teach the team how to play and make sure they understand the rules of the game. Be there to work through tactics, strategies, and problems they run into along the way. When the team goes in to play, you know they will have the skills, knowledge, and backing to go all out.

The most rewarding part of what I do is when I see the employees of my clients, from all different areas of the organisation, step into their individual genius and work in a way they didn't know they were capable of. As an innovation leader, my role is to enable, encourage, train, and make the team the hero of the innovation project. When they deliver, I feel like a proud parent watching the team showcase the outcome of their blood, sweat, and tears. I am proud they have delivered on their vision, and even prouder they are able to replicate the process and teach others how to innovate and deliver.

INNOVATION IS NOT AN EXTRACURRICULAR ACTIVITY

I cannot stress this enough. If you make innovation an extracurricular activity, do not expect any consistent, timely results. Nor can you consider your organisation to have a culture of innovation.

Don't allow innovation to fall into the trap of being an extra-curricular activity for your teams. When this happens, it is very difficult to get a project off the ground because the team's ability to find the time will be limited. Over time, it will be only one or two dedicated people attempting to drive the process forward, and they will feel like they are not getting anywhere. Very rarely are there spare or underutilised resources just waiting around for a new project to work on.

Don't make teams feel like this is a side-hustle or they are being punished by working on an innovation project. Treat it the same way you would any other program of work. Resource it well, provide a reasonable budget, and accommodate this work into each employee's schedule. As outlined in step two, prioritise this work in the organisation and treat it like a self-sustaining portfolio.

If other people in the organisation see that any work on an innovation project is in *addition* to their current workload, and possibly not included in their key performance indicators or annual review, you may find it hard to get the right number of willing volunteers to create a meaningful innovation portfolio. By the very nature of innovation, it's likely to attract proactive, highly motivated self-starters who are often the go-to people for leaders to get stuff done. But we need more than these people in the organisation to create an evolving culture of innovation.

A balance needs to be struck between providing teams and individuals the space and capacity to work on innovation projects and delivering the key programs of work and operational requirements. There are many ways to do this, and the right process will need to be established for your organisation. Be sure to make it inclusive and accessible to everyone. Don't be scared to use people from all over the organisation – those from non-traditional project roles, and those that have no project skills – and give them the opportunity to participate in an innovation project. Give everyone a chance to learn, play, and participate.

Empowering your teams means giving them the skills, space, and tools to be able to make it happen. It is always about 'we' for innovation and never an individual. Trust, collaboration, coaching, and authority to deliver will need to be provided to ensure a sustainable commitment to innovation happens inside your organisation. People are the backbone of any innovation program, and if you don't give them the ability to deliver, they won't.

* * *

Here are the fundamentals of step five:

- Make it as easy and simple as possible for the innovation teams to work through ideas to deliver an outcome.

- Give them a toolkit and then coach and guide them through the process. Remember, as a leader you're a coach, guide and mentor, not the decision-maker.

- Create open feedback processes to ensure there is transparency between the teams and leaders.

- Be comfortable trusting the team to deliver. Make your expectations and non-negotiables clear and let the team go for it.

Step six: incubate

> 'Innovation is the pirate ship that sails into the yacht club.'
> —Lisa Bodell

I know I have spoken about alignment to strategy, building a portfolio, and understanding how to work within the bureaucracy of your organisation. Lots of corporate speak. Well, this section is a little different. Time to shake some of that off. It is at this stage that the freedom to think differently and innovate is required.

Let's have some fun and incubate innovation projects.

GET YOUR BAND OF MISFITS TOGETHER

You have an endorsed idea and you've been given the green light to incubate this idea. Now you'll need a team. Generally I see leaders selecting the highest performers, the most diligent rule followers, who are eager to please and grab that next promotion. *Wrong!* At this point I find it extremely difficult to keep a poker face and hide the enormous eye-rolling moment that's about to happen. Sure, these employees will get the job done. They'll smash out 'something' in the exact time period allocated. Will it be innovative? Who knows? Will it be a break away from the status quo? Probably not.

While these people are sensational employees to have because you can rely on them to get it done, I recommend having no more than one person like this in an innovation team. I refer to these employees as the 'connectors'. They know who to talk to, what process to follow, how to get things done, and the order in which it needs to happen. These people are an essential part of the fabric of the organisation, but you can only have a maximum of one in each innovation team. Their role in the team is important because we need these people to connect the team throughout the organisation and understand the processes and, if appropriate, how to break them.

For a Corporate Innervation Operating System to be effective there needs to be a team of people who question everything. Find the pirates, misfits, rabble rousers, agitators, and black sheep and see who's up for the challenge. Harnessing the creative power of misfits to stir up the status quo can make indelible changes for incredible success. (I am not talking about the recalcitrant, lazy, or excuse-filled people that never deliver on their promises.)

An example of this approach comes from Pixar, and how they shook things up. The story goes that Brad Bird, director of *The Incredibles* and *Incredibles 2* (and many other amazing movies), was brought in to Pixar to shake up the animated movies and take more market share from Disney. There were some incredible (I know – bad pun) nerves around this because his previous project had tanked, and it wasn't his first large failure. Disney had fired him.

Pixar actively chose someone whose previous project was a commercial failure, but it was wildly original, and that is what attracted them. Pixar was conscious that they had the same group of people doing the same things, and while they are unbelievably talented (I mean, who doesn't love *Toy Story*?) they knew they needed to freshen up their thinking.

Brad wrote *The Incredibles* and was bringing his vision to life with the Pixar animation team. The Pixar team developed amazing animations for animals and toys, but their humans were a bit *meh*. A large part of Violet's character was her hair that hung down in her face, to give off that angsty teenage vibe. The computer animation looked terrible – they said it looked like strips of rubber. When they asked what it would take to get it to look like real hair moving, they were quoted 10 years and $10m. These were the star Pixar players saying this!

So off Brad went to hunt down a team of unconventional thinkers within Pixar. Brad searched for the people who had risky ideas that had been overlooked or dismissed. Those people who were frustrated or dissatisfied with how things are. He knew there was no reason to turn to outside consultants because the talent and genius already existed inside Pixar. The frustration and dissatisfaction of the black sheep, rogues, and pirates of Pixar would fuel their creativity and desire to develop a solution. If you've seen the movie *The Incredibles*, you'll know that this team of misfits not only nailed it but they changed the way hair and water is animated. On time and on budget. Mind blown!

The lesson is to look beyond the star players and find the people inside your organisation who are going to challenge the established wisdom. This doesn't have to be a complex process that you need to overthink. To make it a little easier, here is my guide for the six types of innovators you need in your incubation team:

1. **The naysayer, the critic, and the 'yes, but' and 'it won't work because' person.** These people are really uncomfortable with risk. They like to control everything that is in their portfolio and domain. They like to focus on concrete, clear-cut objectives.

   A 'black hat thinker' may come across as initially negative, but this type of approach places a critical check on the thinking that is taking place, and allows the grounding of concepts into rational process. These people are superstars at managing bureaucracy. These people tend not to embrace unstructured environments very well, resulting in them deferring back to the 'tried and true' methodology or solution.

2. **The pirate, black sheep, and misfit.** The unconventional thinkers and those who are dissatisfied with the status quo. Their ideas and suggestions are often overlooked or dismissed because they are different to the way 'things have always been done around here'. These people are not disgruntled with the organisation; in fact, they're committed to the mission. They want to embrace different ideas for the enhancement of the organisation. Harness their frustration to solve problems differently and channel their creativity to develop solutions.

3. **The unicorn hunter.** This person emulates the startups that reach the dizzying heights of a 10-figure valuation. Someone who wants to be the next Uber and has plenty of quotes and stories of how Google and Apple do it, but doesn't and hasn't worked in a startup. These people are plugged into the movements in the market for these types of businesses and are interested in their disruptive process and subsequent success. They will push to be disruptive and will be seeking to shake things up.

4. **The legacy creators.** These people are often seen as the movers and shakers in an organisation. Motivated by KPIs, targets, rewards. Like to influence and lead from the front. They are great when they're on your team, because they push to get things done. Can be a little impatient with their ideas and sometimes this means they leave people behind on the journey. Some people can feel like they are sprinting to keep up with these people. These people have an idea for absolutely everything.

5. **The persistent experimenter.** This person is open to all new ideas, and they believe that anything is possible. Dedicated, hard-working, and often a perfectionist, they will find a way to push through ideas. Persistent in the face of pushback, these people

manage to break down barriers and perceptions that others deemed impossible to change. They are risk-takers and intensely passionate. These people need some boundaries and limits, otherwise they'll continually experiment.

6. **The connector.** These people seem to be good at absolutely everything. Often referred to as a star player. Diligent rule followers, these people know everyone and every step to follow in the precise order. Not only will these people keep the team on track and on time, they'll keep the team within the boundaries of the bureaucracy. And when the process and rules need to be broken, they know who to speak to and which bit to break.

You need a variety of people in your incubation team to make it work. For me the sweet spot is finding one of each of the innovators above and putting them together. Build a team to consider an idea from all angles and watch the magic happen. There may be some initial sparks of friction; stick with it and coach the team through it. The results will be worth it.

To make your incubation team work, it takes a little bit more than just selecting the people and hoping for the best. To get the most out of your innovation incubation team, follow these tips to get your team firing on all cylinders:

- **Form a team of the different types of innovators.** You can have more or fewer people if required, but pay attention to the balance of personalities and types so you get a balance that works for the idea.

- **Disrupters, black sheep, and misfits find each other.** They do tend to flock together so be aware of a self-formed team if it is full of disrupters and black sheep.

- **Gather the team together to hear their frustrations.** Let them be heard. Really see them. If you are really listening to them and helping them constructively air their frustrations, you build a team of allies.

- **Create the common enemy, and I don't mean the middle or senior management.** The enemy may be the status quo that is holding them up, the gap in the market, or the deadline to solve a wicked problem. Get them to focus on this common problem and point them in the right direction. This is the team's mountain to climb together and conquer.

- **Give them an underdog mindset.** It's unbelievable what can happen when people realise the challenge they have in front of them. Chances are they're doing this project with less time, money, and resources than other projects in the organisation. A little bit of competitive tension is healthy to get the creative juices flowing. Being the underdog will also force the team to think differently and do whatever it takes to win. When you have an underdog mindset you don't fear losing, and this removes one of the key blockers.

- **Build a community of support around the team to create, develop, and support ideas and the work they're doing.** Innovation is always a 'we', and it is never about leaving teams isolated to solve the challenges in a black box.

- **Ensure the challenges the team are facing are meaningful, exciting, and not just a burden.** We don't want any incubation team to spin their wheels.

This is not without its risks, but through a controlled and structured process the ability to harness the radically different thinking of some people will create incredible innovation. Your role is to coach and guide the team as they move through this process, and help them collaborate and course correct if necessary.

WAY OF WORKING

There are as many different ways of working as I am tall, and more keep popping up every day. I don't believe in a one-size-fits-all approach – a way of working will need to be developed or adopted to suit your organisation and people. I am not going to recommend one methodology or discuss the pros and cons of the many and varied types of methodologies. I have an open mind about what will work for each organisation, and I generally take the best bits from a variety of methodologies to create a bespoke solution for an organisation.

As I move through a variety of different organisations I generally recommend ways of working based on these four methodologies, to suit the needs of the individual organisation and its culture:

1. An Agile approach is extremely popular in the innovation and development space. This approach utilises cross-functional teams that are flexible to respond to a continually changing environment and arising issues in the development of new ideas.

2. The Lean Startup model is focused on shortened development cycles to move fast into prototyping, and relies on constant experimentation and iterative releases of a proposed solution.

3. Design Thinking or Human-Centred Design focuses on an empathetic approach to the customer to move through an ideation and prototyping process based on the customer.

4. DevOps is an amalgamation of development, operations, and delivery to bring the entire product lifecycle together for design, development, and deployment.

These are all fabulous methodologies. Not one of these methodologies is better than the other. It is important that you make a deliberate choice to select a way of working – whether a pure or hybrid model – that is most likely to lead to success in terms of the environment you are implementing and the people you are asking to use it.

What you need is consistency and a thorough understanding of what and how you want your teams to work. You want all of your incubation teams to work in the same way, although they will be solving different problems and creating different solutions. Be careful about making this too disciplined, as you don't want to stifle the creative process. It needs to be just enough to balance an adaptive, fast, and creative process with the need for budget management, risk management, and reporting mechanisms. Rules are great, but we also need to know when they are just guides and need to be broken. What's important here is consistency.

FLEARNing

It is nothing new to talk about failing fast and failing forward. With the right way of working in place, the checks and balances will be there to ensure a failing project can either be course corrected or halted. We also need to learn from the mistakes we have made, and this applies to successful and failed projects. It is common practice to run a retrospective on a project to understand what worked and didn't work. This is an excellent way for the team to understand their performance and what they will do differently. But what we tend to do is hold onto the information in the team. This information needs to be shared to all people in the organisation so learning can happen at scale.

FLEARNing (learning through failure) is about more than just the project team. This is about celebrating all of the work completed by incubation teams and creating a process for the entire organisation to learn from any failures or mistakes. I say celebrate because this is about understanding that sometimes things don't work but it's not because the team didn't try or did something wrong. It's about sharing all the ideas and learnings along the journey. This requires trust, respect, and an understanding that the organisation acknowledges the work being done to assess new innovation ideas.

It's not just about accepting the impending fail, but learning through it. This is a critical aspect, because you're never too far gone to consider a change because something isn't working. I learnt this lesson very early, not from my experience in the corporate environment but from my love of movies. A movie I love and watched a lot (probably too many times) growing up is *Back To The Future*.

The movie we see today almost didn't happen – Michael J Fox wasn't initially involved. The filmmakers had wanted him for the part of Marty McFly, but Michael was unavailable. So Eric Stoltz was cast as the lead. Eric was a talented young actor who had a lot of hype surrounding him. But five weeks into shooting, director Robert

Zemeckis, executive producer Steven Spielberg, and writer Bob Gale reviewed the footage so far and they had a sinking feeling the movie just wasn't going to work. And it wasn't the script. After some serious soul searching and late-night conversations, they decided that Eric Stoltz didn't have the comic abilities to get the most out of what they knew was a very funny script.

This was a huge problem. They had shot more than half the movie. A plan was hatched and they made a proposition to the studio to allow them to replace Stoltz with their original target, Michael J Fox, who was now available. This was a risky proposition that would require more money, more time, and some quick contract negotiations. If you're a fan of the movie like I am, you know that they got Michael J Fox to play Marty McFly, and the rest is history ...

Holy guacamole, that was a gutsy move! The reason I love this example so much and draw on it in my work is that these people understood that if they were going to give their movie the best shot at being successful they needed to leave their egos at the door and put everything on the table to fix it. They were not fixated on the individual decisions they had made to get to that point, rather as a team they focused on what they needed to do to make it right. They examined their work, they didn't personalise the decisions made, and they put the success of the team and the movie above the individuals. They collectively admitted they had made a mistake, but without blame or repercussions. They just fixed it.

Failing is scary, and no one likes to have it happen to them. It hurts their pride and can really dent their confidence. But we learn significantly more from our failures and mistakes than from any of our successes. It is important to remove the personal and individual relationship to failed innovation projects. To support your incubation teams through this process it is beneficial to coach them through the following thought processes:

- **Don't personalise failure.** This is not part of their personal identity and it doesn't make them a failure. Failing when you have tested concepts, hypotheses, and ideas means that you worked on the best thinking you had at the time and you didn't get your intended outcome. Take the time to focus on what could have been done differently to understand the problem better and hone your decision-making skills.

- **It is not a career-limiting move.** You don't need to start hunting for a new job. Take the lesson. It's what you do with the information you have gained and how you support the learning of the broader organisation that matters. Soak up all the information, learn from it, and apply it next time you have the opportunity.

- **Test and measure.** Learn to continuously test and measure, and give yourself permission to make errors along the way. Not intentionally of course, but through a structured process of trial and error. Knowing what doesn't work can be just as important as knowing what does work.

- **Fail fast.** Like all good working methodologies advocate, don't dig yourself into a hole that you can't get out of. Remove the thinking that you need to double down on what you've already done to ensure you can return something on the time, money, resources, and emotional energy you have already invested. This is known as the 'sunk cost bias', and it's the thing that hooks gamblers and businesses when they try to hold on to a losing strategy because they think it will turn around. Knowing when to pull the pin on a project that's moving in the wrong direction takes courage and a significant amount of emotional intelligence.

- **Don't be afraid to fail.** If you're not challenging and questioning everything in the project, you will not gain the knowledge or success from the project. Inaction is just as much a failure as failing recklessly. Failure is fleeting, as long as you get up, implement the lessons, and try again.

This stage is about understanding how to get the right people together, providing the tools and guidance, then giving them the breathing space to work through concepts and solutions. You can have the most schmicko way of working and foolproof tools to support the teams, but if you don't put the right people together you're unlikely to get the best result. A way of working is just a guidance tool. Think of it like the lane ropes in a swimming pool. They're there to keep the team in their lane and guide them up and down the pool. Lane ropes will keep them on track, but it won't make them a champion swim team.

* * *

Here are the fundamentals of step six:

- Harness the power of a collaborative group of different thinkers. Don't be tempted to fall into old habits of giving the projects to 'the usual suspects'. The right people who push us to think differently and question everything will inevitably help create a much better solution.

- Make unwavering collaboration a non-negotiable of playing in this space.

- Use a way of working that suits your innovation team, corporate environment, and processes. Be consistent.

- FLEARN – learn through failing in a structured environment. Shift the relationship of failure from one that often feels personal to one that is entrenched in a structured process for the betterment of the project.

Step seven: create transparency and open communication

Humanise the process. Tools won't do this for you.

COMMUNICATION

As you have moved through the steps you'll be getting an understanding that successful Corporate Innervation is more about people and communication. My recommended process for communication is provided in the context of implementing the Corporate Innervation Operating System, but this can and probably should apply to all aspects of work.

Your people are your biggest asset, and their ability to engage with the innovation program will determine how successful it will be. The effectiveness of your communications will have a significant impact on how well your teams participate, collaborate, and drive forward a culture of innovation. We want to turn your employees into the super-heroes of innovation, and to do this we need to develop a collaborative process with open and transparent channels.

Success is more than the deployment of ideas that add value to the bottom line. It will be achieved when you have an innovation portfolio and Corporate Innervation Operating System that flourishes through self-formed communities of practice throughout the organisation and a clear spirit of engagement that comes though informed employees. Your employees become a body of knowledge and an essential part of the education process for innovation.

There are tools aplenty for communication, messaging, collaboration, and virtual teams, and it seems there's a new one hitting the market every day. I have worked with many organisations where there were so many communication and collaboration tools that more information was missed than received. Some teams were using Slack, others Teams, Monday, Jira, Confluence, Trello, Azure, DevOps, and many more, all within the one organisation. Not to mention they were also using email and a companywide messenger platform. This often occurs through either a specific set of requirements or a leader's preference for and comfort with a particular tool, but what ends up happening is some people have access to some tools and not others, which can be acceptable for other programs of work but not innovation.

I am not here to question or select the collaboration and communication tools for an organisation, but there needs to be a strategic approach to the tools you use. You need to decide what is best for your organisation, but if you don't make it open and transparent for everyone, you can throw away all your best intentions because you'll be moving into a black box exclusionary process where only selected people can participate.

Select a process and a mechanism and stick with it. Pick something that is relatively simple and straightforward to use. Don't fall into the trap of thinking that because it's for innovation it needs to be super-technical and flashy. The simple tools are often the best. Remember your audience: it's the entire organisation. The skills and abilities you are catering for will vary quite significantly, and you will need to focus on the lowest skillset to make sure everyone feels comfortable using it.

When you have open and transparent communication, your employees will see the complete end-to-end journey of each idea. This becomes part of the knowledge development process as the ideas, process, decisions, lessons, and outcomes are constantly available for the entire organisation to see.

TRANSPARENCY

Transparency engenders trust. Trust is an integral element in the Corporate Innervation Operating System because the employees are trusting you with their ideas, and how you deal with them will determine the engagement and long-term viability of the program.

What does it really mean to have transparent communication? It means:

- **Open and honest communication.** It's not going to be easy and you're not always going to get it right, but you need to get in front of your office grapevine and become the first and single source of truth for innovation. This is mutually beneficial for employees and leaders. You're showing respect, courtesy, and acknowledgement that every employee is crucial to the Corporate Innervation Operating System. Your employees will feel valued, and it will support collaboration and development of an innovation culture. Many of us have worked for organisations where amazing things have happened but we've read about it in the press or seen it on social media after the event. Happens every day, and it doesn't feel good for the employees. Lead from the front when it comes to communications and you will show all members of the organisation the behaviour and level of trust you expect in the innovation function.

- **No secrets.** Let's leave the *wow* moments to the incubation teams. There will always be a requirement for decisions to be made, and some of these decisions people will not agree with. That's okay. Don't let the rumour mill start. Always be on the front foot and be transparent about all decisions. Make the decision, minutes, and process of the innovation investment committee available to everyone.

- **Everyone can see and be a part of the conversation.** Transparency isn't just about keeping everyone informed. We want people to see the ideas, challenges, stumbling points, and wicked problems because they may have an idea to help along the way. You don't know what you don't know, and someone looking at a problem or idea from a different perspective may be able to fill in some of the blanks or support the solution development. You want feedback, support, troubleshooting, and testing help throughout the entire business. Not everyone can be in the incubation team, but they can support the team along the way.

- **No ambiguity.** Sometimes it's not what you say, but what you *don't* say. Make it simple, make it clear, and make it consistent. Skip the jargon, buzzwords, and other corporate speak or acronyms you have in your organisation. Instead of feeling like I need to adapt to the different vernacular in all the organisations I work with, I just remove it. These unique dialects are nothing but exclusionary. I can't tell you the number of times I have asked someone to explain an acronym used in their organisation and they haven't been able to. They are exclusionary because often people are too shy to ask what it means; no one wants to lose face by appearing not to know something among their peers. If you want everyone on the same page fast, remove all acronyms from your communications and conversations. Make a swear jar for when people use them. It makes a nice little earner for a charity of your choice. Once you have broken the habit, your communications will be clearer and you will remove a lot of ambiguity.

- **Open feedback loops.** Create open feedback loops to hear from your audience and ensure that they understand, are getting information that's meaningful to them, and they're able to participate in the process.

Make your communication timely, frequent, and consistent. Leverage the leaders, champions, and influencers in your organisation to make it more effective. Be authentic, inclusive, and open to a two-way conversation.

* * *

Here are the fundamentals of step seven:

- Humanise the process of communication and remove your reliance on an abundance of tech tools.

- Whatever mechanism you choose for communication, make it consistent, timely, and transparent.

- Be transparent, open, and honest.

- Include everyone in the conversation.

Step eight: monetise

*Time to stop hoping you will monetise and **know** that you will.*

Innovation is one of the most important factors of growth, and now you have a great way of finding the genius inside your organisation and helping people create and implement ideas for growth, efficiency, and increased profit. The focus on innovation has conditioned the thinking of too many people to have a 'build it and they will come' mentality. They justify this thinking through the stories of Harry Potter, Netflix, Google, and Nutmeg that despite their rejections at the start of their journey, they were successful beyond even their own expectations. Yes, they are incredible case studies, but they are the exception and not the rule.

The failure rate for innovations is hideously high, with almost 75% of implemented innovations missing their profit or defined success target. The Corporate Innervation Operating System is not an exact science but a framework that guides your thinking processes so that it will set you up for success.

Monetising is hard, and it never gets easy. The benefit you will be cognisant of by now is that by following and implementing the Corporate Innervation Operating System you are doing the ground-work first to ensure you can monetise your innovation portfolio.

In the corporate context you will have monetised your innovation when it has met or exceeded the defined financial goals you have agreed upon. This may be in the form of revenue for a new product or cost savings for efficiency-style ideas. Where you have intangible benefits, create metrics that you can effectively measure to understand your success, or areas you need to improve on.

There are countless models for monetising innovation, and this could easily be a book all of its own. As such, I am going to give an overview of how I see it and the steps I take and coach my clients through. I have been successfully monetising startups, corporate innovations, and my own businesses since 2012 and have been successfully using the steps I outline below. This won't give you all the answers, but it will help you understand the complexity of monetisation and provide you with the areas to focus on to be successful.

It is affirming to see that monetising – and understanding how to do it effectively – is a huge body of work in both the academic and consultancy space. There's no shortage of information for you to read and learn from, and a lot of it follows a similar commonsense process. This topic is big and meaty.

So why do so many innovations miss their defined success targets?

Monetising is difficult, strategic, and requires consistent effort. This is after you've gone through the hard slog of conceptual development, build, and implementation ... now you have to make it sing.

There are lots of reasons why you may be unable to monetise your newly minted innovation, notwithstanding external market factors which you may not be able to predict let alone control. I'm going to focus on the key areas that you *can* control in your business and issues you can – with any luck – avoid. Here is my take on what I know works to monetise innovation in a corporate environment.

AVOID THE 'EVERYTHING BUT THE KITCHEN SINK' IDEA

To ensure you will be able to monetise your innovation you must be thinking about your end customer throughout the entire process. Your product needs to be able to articulate a clear value proposition. A one-size-fits-all approach rarely, if ever, works. Clearly, this is something that cannot wait until the end. By then it's too late.

The 'everything but the kitchen sink' idea is the product or service that has been over-engineered with every possible feature, and may even include the kitchen sink (kidding not kidding). You know the ones. These are reveals where you almost take a step back with eyebrows raised when you see the final showcase because it has an overwhelming number of features. You almost ask yourself if there is anything it *can't* do.

Often, the customer has a different experience. In fact, it's the opposite of a wow moment for them. All they can see are the features they are unlikely to use. Instead of feeling like they would get great value, the item will feel overpriced because why would they want a product they may only use 5% or 10% of? Clearly this is something that needs to be thought through from the get-go.

One of my favourite ways to illustrate this to teams is the fictional example of the car designed by Homer Simpson. On the hunt for the car that all Americans would want to drive to beat the Japanese car companies, a car company believes that Homer understands the needs and wants of the average American car owner.

In short, Homer is given a blank slate to design and build the car 'every American would want'. What ensues is a monstrosity of a car with everything that a car owner probably *doesn't* need, like bubble domes and muzzles for the kids, shag carpet, three different types of horns ... and the list of stupidity goes on. This is also an obnoxiously expensive vehicle to make, which sends the company to the wall because no one in their right mind wants to buy a car like that.

I know this is a far-fetched and fictional parody (it is *The Simpsons*), but when we are emotionally attached to an idea it's easy to lose perspective and aim to add that extra wow factor with too many 'things'. This is a great example because I get teams to stick a picture of Homer's car on the wall and look at it every day when they are considering not only the end user but the features of the product.

The section on 'walking in their shoes' is paramount to the success of the uptake by your current and potential customers. To help avoid this mistake I suggest you pin up a picture of Homer Simpson's car and some pictures and profiles of your ideal customers so you can put their needs front and centre through every step of the innovation process.

GETTING YOUR PRICING RIGHT

Finding the sweet spot of the correct price for your innovation is definitely easier said than done, so it's worth dedicating the time and effort to construct a pricing strategy to support its market entry. Remember, price is the only component of your marketing strategy that can generate revenue, and it is often the key driver of perceived value. It's too easy to get distracted at this point by the bright, shiny, and fun aspects of marketing. Stay focused on understanding what the customer is willing to pay and building a model to understand the fixed and floating costs throughout the lifecycle of the innovation to ensure you can achieve your monetisation targets.

Underpricing

If you underprice your new innovation there is the possibility that you will never give it the opportunity to reach its full potential. Cheap doesn't always equate to good value. It can lead to a perception of lower quality if your competitors are more expensive than you. It is soul-destroying to bring to market an innovation that meets, and possibly exceeds, customer expectations, but because it is undervalued you have underexploited the opportunity.

I understand the logic here … deliberately offer a lower price, or sometimes free, in order to boost demand and seek to capture a greater share of the market. It is often thought that this will attract attention and a mass of customers and demand beyond your wildest expectations. This strategy often fails for two reasons:

- You may have failed to differentiate your product enough.
  The perceived value of your product will be determined by
  the market comparisons your customers make. Why will your
  customers value this in the same way? Why will they change if
  there's no perceived additional value or benefit?

- Is this an innovation that cannot demand a higher price, despite
  all the research, development, and work that has been put into it?
  If this is the case, it's unlikely that you will be able to truly realise
  the value and monetise your innovation, despite being the right
  product for the market at the right time.

Overpricing

This strategy can dramatically backfire, but it occasionally works. Creating a premium pricing process seems like it might be a good idea to elevate the status of your innovation to be higher than your immediate competition. But a higher price doesn't always mean higher quality.

For this to work there needs to be a delicate balance of factors in play. This strategy can only be successful if there is price-inelastic demand for what you are selling that is coupled with a bulletproof unique selling proposition (USP). When you tick the box on both of those factors, you will also require brand equity and brand reputation that instils trust to allow your customers to feel good about paying a premium price.

When you have all these factors and you want to go for a premium pricing model, it can still limit your ability to successfully monetise by:

- Limiting your ability to sell to the mass market. Premium pricing models are generally for niche markets. If this is a broader consumer product you may be voluntarily pricing out a large section of your market.

- Being undercut by your competitors or analogous products in the market. If your market is crowded, you are truly not unique, or are easily replicable, your competitors will be out there selling a cheaper equivalent and capturing your declining market share.

- Your development, maintenance, and marketing costs are likely to be higher over the lifecycle of your innovation because a small customer base may have larger fixed costs and higher probability of losses early in the stages of the customer relationship. With a smaller customer base it takes longer to move into a positive relationship between profitability and lifecycle of customers. You have to establish if you can manage that process and if the profitability will be worth the possible up-front losses.

In many instances pricing seems to be a set-and-forget process. The pricing component of your monetisation strategy needs to be a continuous test and measure process throughout its entire lifecycle.

BRING THE DECISION-MAKERS ON THE JOURNEY

It's no secret that large organisations struggle with innovation, not only from a development and process perspective, but also from an unwillingness to take the risks to realise the potential value of an innovation.

This can happen when there is a disconnect between the executive leadership team and the team developing the innovation, and so the new idea never makes it to market. These innovations are backlogged, overlooked, or it's just bad timing, but the value is never realised because they do not see the light of day. There can be many reasons for this, including:

- an underlying change in strategy

- an executive team unable to recognise or agree with the potential value of the innovation

- tensions around the risk tolerances for this innovation make it unpalatable

- not being willing to bear the initial losses for potential long-term value realisation

- organisational change is hard

- no leader is willing to take the risk.

This is a difficult and challenging one to move through, because in large organisations these decisions are often made around shareholder value. Innovations that challenge the thinking of executives and the board often require a new or different business model to be successful. Your organisation is generally structured to deliver on the current business model to achieve the objectives of the strategic plan. It can be this myopic view that stops an innovation dead in its tracks.

There's no easy answer or guaranteed solution. I recommend engaging the executive leadership team and, if appropriate, the board early in the conversation to keep them engaged. You need an ally at the table when these ideas are being discussed, voted on, and prioritised. For ideas that are really going to test the business model or are possibly transformational, I have engaged a board member as one of the sponsors of the project, in addition to a member of the executive team. I have had a number of raised eyebrows around both the board table and executive leadership team, but as an innovation leader I know how hard it is to change a mindset that doesn't want to change. Bring the decision-makers on the journey.

Use this recommendation sparingly; you really want to save this for the transformational ideas that are going to push people's thinking.

WALKING DEAD PROJECTS

You can create what you believe is the greatest innovation on the planet but if there is no demand then this really becomes a walking dead idea. These are the ones that raise an eyebrow because the market is questioning how this idea even made it to development. Demand for the innovation is virtually non-existent.

How does this happen? There are many reasons – these are just the most common:

- The innovation was conceptualised and developed in a black box, without any thought to understand the potential customer. In a nutshell, this is trying to solve a non-existent problem for potential customers. Why would people pay for something they don't need, want, or understand?

- Your innovation and development team are too emotionally attached to the project and are no longer realistic or objective about the commercial outcome.

- You've stopped questioning the market viability of your innovation and you can hear yourself saying, 'we've come too far … we can't back out now … '.

There are countless examples of walking dead corporate innovation ideas – a quick Google search will show you a staggering number. One that always makes me giggle is the Evian Water Bra. Wait … what? *Why?* Who knows what they were thinking, but they clearly weren't talking to their customers. In 2005 Evian created a water-filled bra to supposedly help keep women cool in the summer months, and it even featured a small pouch to hold a bottle of Evian mineral water.

Evian clearly did not take a spin in their customers' shoes (or bras) to understand what women really want. The reaction on launch was, 'what were they *thinking*?' This product was rapidly removed, and I'm sure the team at Evian would like to forget it ever existed. Unfortunately, an intended transformational product that bad becomes a case study in what *not* to do.

RULES FOR MONETISATION

I like to keep this as simple as possible, because really that's how it should be. People buy ideas, products, and services, so the crux of this section is to make it easy and compelling for them to do so. Let me say that again ... *make it easy and compelling for them to do so.* Monetisation is more than just another strategy – it needs to be a dynamic process that is continually reviewed and evolving. Your buyers are savvy and operating in a market where they are saturated with choices.

The following are inherently simple concepts, but don't kid yourself because the implementation is difficult. I see so many teams come so far on the journey of implementation and stumble on this last stage. It's not because they're fatigued, but because they're excited, energised, and oftentimes too close to the project to be objective enough.

Your go-to-market strategy

Bringing a product or service to market requires a well-thought-out plan in the form of a go-to-market strategy. You've spent all that time on ideation, conceptualising, and development – don't fall over at the last hurdle. The purpose of this process is to develop an integrated marketing and sales plan that is intended to be a playbook for how you will deliver the unique value proposition to achieve your monetisation goals.

I know I have continually asked you to stop thinking like a startup, but this is the one time when I *do* want you to act more like a startup and less like a big corporate. Startups rely on generating interest and building inbound sales funnels to maximise their ability to convert sales, and therefore monetise their activities. They sweat every asset they have to optimise the performance of their innovation in the market, and you need to do the same, with the broader consideration for the overarching roadmap and brand of the organisation.

Please don't throw this over the fence for your marketing team to do for you. The best and most effective go-to-market strategies are built collaboratively with the development team, sales people, and marketing experts. All the research, vision, process, and knowledge that you have gained through the development process needs to be consolidated into a plan that can be leveraged for growth.

(If you are launching an internal product or process, don't bypass this step. It's easy to think you don't need this and jump straight into a change-management framework, but you need to remember your internal customers are as important as your external customers. Your new customers may not be buying this product in the same way but you are looking to maximise their engagement, and this is a great blueprint for understanding the best way to do this.)

There are a number of ways to put together a go-to-market strategy, but I find the most effective strategy will focus on:

- **Who is your customer?** Know who your customer is and develop buyer personas for your customers. You need to see through your potential customers' eyes to ensure you know how to target them effectively.[3] Having buyer personas is nothing new, particularly for professional marketers, but instead of creating personas from market research, the focus needs to be on understanding the problems they need to solve and the process they go about to solve them. This is more than thinking in the language of the customer to tailor a personalised message, but rather understanding the journey of the different personas and where they intersect to build a strategic approach to understanding the problem to be solved. The qualitative and quantitative work you have done in the 'walk in their shoes' section can be redeployed and built upon to create an understanding of the buyer personas you need to work through, which are:

  - the initiator
  - the influencer
  - the decision-maker

3   I read the book *Buyer Personas: How to gain insight into your customer's expectations, align your marketing strategies, and win more business* in 2015 and was inspired to rethink how I go about understanding who my buyer is and how they are influenced. I highly recommend this book.

- the approver
- the buyer
- the gatekeeper
- the user.

- **How will your customer buy?** Make it easy to buy. It really needs to be as simple as that. Once you know who your customer is and the potential gatekeepers they need to move through, do everything you can to make it as easy and simple as possible to buy. If you are selling B2B and you understand the gatekeepers like procurement, see if you can develop the mechanisms to smooth this process. Likewise, if you are 'selling' to internal customers, make it easy to access. This is often a forgotten aspect of the go-to-market process with the greater focus on marketing, but we need to consider this: if we have the snazziest and greatest marketing in the world but it's difficult for the customer to buy, you're not going to get as many customers as possible. It's of the utmost importance that you work with your marketing team when building the sales process. These clever cookies can help you with their internal and external market knowledge of your customers, and this will support them in building the marketing plan and collateral.

- **Know what your customers will pay.** This needs to be thought through early in the process. You also need to be willing to have the conversations with your potential customers or users about their propensity to pay, to understand their sensitivities and the price elasticity of demand in this market. You can generate hype, interest, and a funnel of interested people, but if your item is priced beyond what they are willing to pay, you will be unlikely to leverage this opportunity to show how your innovation matches their needs.

- **Have a pricing strategy.** This is your articulation of the method you have chosen to maximise shareholder value and profits, while seeking to hit the sweet spot between market and consumer demand. Whatever methodology or process you have used to determine your price, it should never be a set-and-forget exercise. You need to consider how you will price your innovation over its entire lifecycle. If an innovation has successfully launched and is gaining a stable market share and revenue, I often see the team breathe a huge sigh of relief and move on to either the operationalisation of the innovation or another project. But just as your innovation requires consistent fine tuning and optimisation, so does your pricing. Your market is not static, and you need to continually analyse and understand the interdependence of internal and external variables that can impact the way you price, to allow you to move with the market and aim to capture maximum value over the long term.

- **Have a marketing plan** which will include all the usual suspects of an overview of the competitive landscape, SWOT, content and message matrix, sources of marketing, inbound automation tools, and anything else suited to your project. Work collaboratively with your marketing team – don't delegate this key piece out and hope for the best. Your marketing team are the experts for marketing, and your team have become the experts for your innovation and your potential customers, so you need to join forces and work collaboratively on the marketing plan. Like pricing, this is not a set-and-forget plan. Have a focus on optimisation to ensure you maximise the number of customers entering and moving through the sales funnel you have designed. Test and measure the content you are creating to understand how it performs against your buyer personas, and continually adapt to optimise the performance of your marketing efforts.

- **Who will do the selling?** Do you know how you will convert and sell your innovation? Will your customer respond better to a marketing-intensive or sales-intensive process? Sales and marketing are counterbalances, and knowing this will allow you to plan your resources accordingly. In theory, the more effort you put into marketing the less intensive the sales approach required, and vice versa. Once you have determined this, you can use it to determine the resourcing required. Don't forget to communicate your sales strategy to your marketing team so they can build this into their marketing plan, content, and collateral.

- **Will a support team be required?** Will your customers require the support and assistance of a team to help them troubleshoot any issues? There's nothing worse for a customer than completing a transaction and then not having any support later. Support isn't just to get your customers onboard, it's about supporting them through their entire lifecycle with you and your product. It's likely there will always be a new, shinier, and better solution than the one you have in market, but if your customers are loyal to you it can make it hard for them to change. The Iconic is an exceptional example of how to do this well. If something isn't right or you just have some questions, you can email, phone, or use their online chat service. From my personal experience it is fast, friendly, and the staff get to the issue quickly and just solve it.

- **Identify where this sits in the overall roadmap for the division or organisation.** Your innovation cannot be built, managed, and operated in a silo. It's part of a much bigger picture, and consideration needs to be given to how it fits into the broader context of the organisation. As discussed earlier, disruption often creates cannibalisation of another area of the organisation, and we need to ensure alignment with the brand, vision, and strategy of the organisation. It's expected that this will form part of a larger portfolio of offerings to your customers, and you do not want to provide any inconsistent or divergent messages to your customers.

- **Agree on success and benefits realisation metrics.** Agree from the get-go how you are going to measure your success and benefits of this innovation, and build in a reporting process. Align this with the benefits realisation process of your organisation to create synergies and ease of reporting. Don't rely on just a revenue, profit, or take-up rate metric to suffice. They are all too easily taken out of context and won't help you grow over time. I work with my teams to map their success and benefits metrics against internal and external markets to support a true health check. This will help you understand if you are outperforming, underperforming, or on par with the market. Build metrics and a reporting process that will allow you to be as proactive as possible, rather than just placing a number in a monthly report.

- **Articulate the ongoing resources and budget required post launch and in year one.** Plan early for the resources and budget you will need beyond the first year of your innovation. It can be a little too easy to hand a project over to an operational team once it's business-as-usual work, and not continuously move through the areas of the Corporate Innervation Operating System that will assess and reassess your innovation and performance in the market.

Okay, now that you have a go-to-market strategy, don't file that document away and let it gather dust. This is your living and breathing plan for continually engaging with the market. Review this, and test and measure everything and refine. Your go-to-market strategy will only be successful if you work it.

Your customers and people are not homogenous

Market segmentation should be a core component of your marketing plan in your go-to-market strategy, but I want to put some more emphasis on this to acknowledge the importance of knowing your buyers will want to feel that you are speaking to them in their language. If you have gone through a buyer's journey process you will realise there are seven people – buyers – you need to talk to in order to convert a sale. (These were given above.)

Segment according to your findings in the buyer's journey process. I often see teams try to 'make fit' the customer segments from the organisation overall into their go-to-market strategy, because it's expected to use the segmentation provided by the marketing team. The broader organisational segmentation will provide an excellent starting point, but it's worth doing the extra steps here because your customers may not be exactly the same. Or if they are, the way they approach this issue or problem to solve may be different, and we need to talk to them in a way that engages them.

Jobs to be done

In step four of the framework I asked you to walk in a customer's shoes and understand their propensity to be irrational and emotional buyers, which is why there often isn't a strong correlation between what they say they will do and what they actually do. Often the reason for this is the dozens of small but important other decisions and changes that may need to be made if they are to buy your innovation. This is where the needs of the buyer must be analysed against their behaviour to understand what they will do to get the job done.

'Jobs to be done' is a well-documented marketing framework that has its roots in customer-centred design. Understanding the 'jobs to be done' of your buyers will allow you to categorise, define, and prioritise the needs of your buyers. In putting together the conceptual framework for your innovation, it is highly likely that you have thought through these to determine if you are solving a problem or creating a 'nice to have'. Utilising the knowledge and thought you have put into the design process to create a solution for your innovation will help you bring all the pieces together when you talk to your customer in the sales process.

Using the need statements, insights, and emotional irrationality of customers all together in a framework will help you navigate through the crowded markets and information overload in order to talk to your buyers in a way that makes sense to them. The intersection between 'jobs to be done' and your 'buyer's journey' will help anchor your marketing and sales process to target your potential buyers at the point where the innovation creates value. This is where your team can talk about the 'desired outcomes' of the buyer in a way that is measurable and able to be realised.

This is an imperative part of the thinking and planning process for monetisation, because this knowledge needs to be integrated across all people interacting with this innovation going to market. Your marketing, sales, operations, support, and management all need to be focused on the same results to ensure end-to-end consistency and outcomes that surprise and delight your buyers, not just focus on function.

Maintaining integrity on price

You've done the work on your price structure and you've built a model to consider the variables and you've created sales or revenue targets for your team. The moment of truth arrives, and your sales figures don't match your forecasts or the trends in the market. What do you do? You've been in the market for one or two quarters and you are getting concerned about what you are going to do to increase sales.

What you are *not* going to do is lower the price. Why? That sends a conflicting message to the market: your innovation really is worth less than the price you placed on it. There is a real downside to price reductions and it's worth thinking these through:

- The market may think you were trying to hoodwink them with an innovation that is not of the quality you profess it to be. This can hurt your brand integrity and the trust equation you have with your customer.

- The market will see this as a statement of what the innovation is really worth and therefore what they really should be paying.

- It suggests there is not a great deal of confidence in your innovation.

- It will significantly erode your profit margin over time.

- It reduces the lifetime value of a buyer.

What do you do? Go back to the people on your team looking after sales, marketing, and strategy to look at and rethink the value proposition, jobs to be done, and language that you are using with your potential buyers. Talk to your potential buyers and find out why they are not making the leap to purchase. Look at all the non-price factors to understand if you have a problem you need to fix. Focus on:

- Does the market or buyer understand what you are selling? Do they need more information or do you need to change the way you communicate?

- Is it too similar to a competitor item, or did they undercut your price?

- Does it not meet the needs of your buyer?

- Does the sales process need to change?

- Do you have a quality problem?

Going to market is a nerve-wrecking experience. Not only are you seeking broader acceptance from your target market, but you have the added pressure of meeting the success metrics you have established for this innovation. Don't be tempted to rush in and reduce the price to get a quick shot of sales. You need to play the long game here and know that you are looking to build a market for your innovation. Remember, price adjustments cannot fix quality, features, support, or any other non-price components of the process.

RISK PARTICIPATION PARTNERSHIPS

There are many different permutations of why you may look to partner up on the development or distribution of your innovation. In some instances you will create and develop an innovation that is outside the core focus of your business. Or you may have an idea that has the potential to create incredible value for your organisation but you do not have the resources or capability in-house to bring it to life. For some ideas the level of risk may be beyond the tolerances the organisation is comfortable with and require a different solution.

I have seen many ideas diluted in the market when external consultants have managed the 'build' of the idea. If an entirely new process has been created then how does the organisation isolate that development knowledge, IP, and secret sauce from the rest of the world? Contracts and non-disclosure agreements are fantastic but our awesome human brains will have trouble forgetting and putting an ethical wall around what has been learned.

Often this is unintentional, with no malice, but human nature shows that it is impossible to unsee or unknow something once we have created it. The people who do the building and development will inadvertently use that knowledge because it will be almost impossible for them not to. I am not trying to scare you away from using consultants, or say that everything must be done in-house. Rather, I am asking you to think about the 1% of ideas that are so new, different, the potential game-changers that you may want to consider a different risk and monetisation model to secure your proprietary IP.

One of the ways to support this process and isolate some of the risks associated with partnering and monetisation of an innovation is to utilise a special purpose vehicle (SPV) that legally separates the assets, innovation, and risks from the parent company. There are many different ways to structure an SPV, and the purpose of this section is not to get into the detail of how to structure an SPV, but rather to provoke a conversation around the possibility of this being an option.

For these one-percenters it's worth locking up the IP and getting the people who help you either build or monetise to put some skin in the game and partner with you. Guns for hire are great to get some work done, but no one works harder than someone who will benefit from the final result. There are also some key benefits outside of engagement, including:

- protecting vulnerable intellectual property

- bringing in outside expertise without the risk of loss of IP

- possible access to new and different buyers of the innovation

- the ability to attract outside investors

- an exit strategy can be easily defined.

Organisations shy away from partnering or SPV structures for a number of different reasons, all of them valid, but in my experience it comes down to the assumption that they will be unable to control the entity and effectively manage any potential brand risk. An SPV with an external partner can be difficult to get right, but it also can be an incredible success if time, thought, and the right legal and financial minds come together to create the rules of engagement.

There are many ways to do this – I tell my clients that they need to think of it like a marriage. Get a watertight pre-nuptial agreement so that everything you owned going into the 'marriage' is yours and any joint assets created during the life of the agreement will be split according to the agreed percentage of ownership going into the agreement. Rarely are couples friends after they divorce, and it's generally the same for business partnerships, so plan for the worst and hope for the best.

Monetising is hard and takes a huge amount of effort. Don't underestimate how much time you need to dedicate to this part of the process. If you want to successfully monetise your innovation you need to continually revisit and cycle through these steps. It is a never-ending process of testing, measuring, refinement, and optimisation. It is never a set-and-forget process.

* * *

Fundamentals of step eight:

- Every aspect of your monetisation process needs to start and finish with the customer at the centre of your thinking.

- Your pricing structure is not a set-and-forget process – think of this as something that requires continual review and management.

- Don't delegate out sales and marketing to the respective teams. Join forces and create a collaborative team to build a go-to-market strategy that utilises the collective wisdom of the experts and acquired knowledge of the innovation team.

- Consider alternative risk and delivery models when there is the potential risk of IP loss on unique ideas.

Step nine: avoid the snap back

You're developing more than just incredible innovation ideas. You are creating a culture of innovation, and it will need constant attention to change behaviours, attitudes, and habits throughout the entire organisation.

I call this the 'rubber band syndrome', because change can be uncomfortable, messy, and it certainly isn't linear. When people become really uncomfortable the rubber band snaps back and people revert to the behaviours and the way they did things before.

You need to measure yourself against your progress goals versus where you really are at a point in time, and assess whether the behaviours match the desired outcome. Be brutally honest with yourself. Improvement can only occur if we're willing to hold a mirror up to ourselves and look at what is really there. All issues need to be acknowledged and dealt with quickly.

Keep your finger on the pulse and implement the following steps to support the ongoing development of innovation:

1. **Constant check-ins.** Using both formal and informal communication methods, talk to anyone and everyone about the Corporate Innervation Operating System so you can understand the sentiment inside the organisation. You want to know the good, bad, and ugly of what's happening, and you will not always get this from formal feedback loops. The watercooler chat, casual coffee, and informal conversations will help you understand what is working and what's not. You need to get among it and hear what everyone is saying and contrast this against their actions.

2. **Leverage leadership, champions, and influencers.** Make sure you are using your support network and advocates to deliver a consistent message for innovation. Your greatest asset is your people. Let innovation become theirs.

3. **Continually build upon the vision and goals of innovation.** Not a stale and static document, but a communication tool to discuss the purpose of innovation. Your message needs to be

aligned with the outcomes of the innovation portfolio. If it's not, you need to think about your messaging and adjust it. It's okay to change. Just be clear, and communicate early and constantly.

4. **Make sure your communications and process really are transparent.** Continually test and measure yourself. Make sure you really have a transparent process. People will tell you, so make sure you ask them.

5. **Celebrate the wins, losses, and milestones along the way.** Celebrate and communicate the achievements of the teams throughout their incubation journey. Remember, you are making the ideas and the people working on them the heroes of innovation.

I work on my own theory of thirds. Quickly identity the top third of people who are enthusiastic, early adopters, and supportive of the process. Encourage them and find the influencers and champions inside this group. Get these people on board early, and they will help you create the shift. Encourage them, get them working on projects, give them tools, and they will be amazing advocates for you and the Corporate Innervation Operating System.

Look around the organisation and talk to people to get a feel for who the people are who *don't* believe in innovation, are cynical towards the process, or who distrust the leadership team and the organisation. Sometimes these people hunt in packs, so if you find a few you may find a larger group, and they're just a little quiet. I refer to this group as the 'bottom third' of change. This is the group that requires the most attention.

Talk to the various people you have identified in the bottom third. Understand their concerns and really hear what they have to say. Keep it constructive, because this is not a whinge fest, nor an opportunity to attack anyone personally. It won't happen straight away but you want the people in the bottom third to be your allies. They may not ever be your cheerleaders, and that's okay. But you do need them focused and on board with the process.

You can't expect to change behaviour when someone is sitting on the sidelines. You need to bring some people from the bottom third all the way into your incubation teams and community. Give them a voice, a project, and something really meaningful to deliver. Their wisdom, knowledge, and work will be appreciated and form part of a solution to an innovation project. Generally, people in this group are not recalcitrant, they're just cynical because they've seen so many different programs and new ways of doing this come and go. You need to show them this is here to stay and you mean business.

If you can grab the hearts and minds of some people in the bottom third, they will become your biggest advocates and supporters of the Corporate Innervation Operating System. The middle third isn't forgotten because there will be a push from the bottom up when you convert the thinking of the bottom third, and a pull through from the top third as their energy, enthusiasm, and efforts will pull people on the journey.

Maintaining any organisational change is hard. It is not easy to make it stick. You need to know where and how to focus your efforts. You are reshaping how you consider new ideas in the organisation and how you deliver on them. It's not a small change, but it's a critical one to the growth and development of your organisation and people.

Keep the rubber band taut, and don't let it snap back.

* * *

Fundamentals of step nine:

- You need to be talking to people and listening to their feedback to ensure that your strategy and daily practices are aligned.

- This is not a linear process, and it's not always going to be easy. Understand there will be ups and downs along the way and use your community, influencers and champions to support the ongoing development and growth of the Corporate Innervation Operating System inside your organisation.

- There's never going to be an opportunity to rest on your laurels because you need to keep the momentum, process and communication rubber band taut so it can't snap back and let people slip into the 'old ways'.

10

What it looks like when you get it right

So, that's a lot of information, processes, and steps to implement. It really is a lot to take in. It's a big framework with a lot of information.

When you have a Corporate Innervation Operating System working inside your organisation you will see:

- a humanised process that puts your people at the centre of the innovation function
- a simplified business model for innovation that is removing the complex and focusing on the value
- a balanced portfolio of exploration and exploitation
- the ability to play the long game, stay relevant, and work on the solutions your internal and external customers really need
- a culture of high-performing teams that are able to weather any storm through their ability to be adaptive, open-minded, and collaborative
- ideas that add value to the bottom line
- a self-sustaining process that's able to have a continuing funnel of ideas and a return on investment that pays for the development of future ideas.

Decide right now what you want innovation to look like inside your organisation, and know that this framework is available to implement and improve on every day as the skills and knowledge of your people develop and grow.

As I was writing this book, along came a pandemic that really put everything in a spin. The dreaded coronavirus (or coronapocalypse, as my daughter calls it) could have ended many innovation programs for lots of organisations. And for many it did. Those that were opportunistic, unstructured, and unable to deliver value were quickly turned off. Projects were put on the shelf, and in some instances teams were let go. I watched as some innovation budgets shrank rapidly, and completely vanished in other cases.

And then I held my breath as my team and I doubled down with our clients to help them through these unprecedented circumstances.

When everything went south with programs of work being cancelled, revenue dropping, people unable to work, a shift to home-working, and fear and uncertainty spreading throughout the economy, I saw all the innervation teams step up and drive the process forward. For these companies, while they had their issues, their innervation teams really stepped up and supported the organisation with:

- access to a portfolio of considered, prioritised ideas – some of these ideas and concepts had been completely developed but the timing wasn't right for implementation

- the ability to quickly implement this framework to activate ideas that could help stem the loss of revenue

- a prioritisation process to rapidly shut down projects and change the focus to work on projects

- an investment and funds allocation process to rapidly deploy funds to programs and projects that were required to support the organisation

- the ability to redeploy human resources from projects and work that was unable to continue, to other programs of work and projects

- leaders, champions, and a community that quickly engaged areas of the organisation that had their work put on hold, and coached and mentored them through new and different projects

- the ability to deploy and go to market with projects and solutions to bring in additional revenue (within three weeks for one solution)

- a culture of innovation, collaborative, and system thinkers that are able to take ideas from concept to final product.

Their Corporate Innervation Operating System had become more than a way of working and processing. It had become part of the soul of the organisation.

To be fair, the coronavirus pandemic took everyone by surprise, and no one really knew what to do. We may have had something like this in our risk management plans, but we never really expected it to happen. While we were all gathered as boards and leadership teams to move through crisis planning and management, the innervation teams were getting on with the job.

The skills and knowledge they had gained through the Corporate Innervation Operating System equipped them to deal with and manage the uncertainty, risk, and messiness of an undefined and yet-to-be-solved problem. Their skills directed their behaviour to create opportunities where we may not have been able to see them through the lens of a crisis.

It is bigger than the individuals. Bigger than the concept of innovation. These organisations have more than an innovation program. They have a culture of system thinkers, collaborators, and coaches that will drive the organisation forward.

This is just the beginning. I am just getting started on Corporate Innervation, and so are you.

WHAT COMES AFTER THE WAVE OF CORPORATE INNERVATION?

The are many challenges facing innovation in the corporate environment, but we need to make sure the top-down corporate structure driven by short-term revenue demands to meet the needs of shareholders and stock prices isn't one of them. Corporate innovation will always struggle to compete with emerging businesses and startups when they are playing in a game that has different rules.

We need to rethink how we activate innovation in the corporate space. It's time to change the game you are playing and focus on the strengths of being a corporate. The next wave of corporate innovation isn't about the next way of working, a technology tool, or new forms of skunklabs to develop ideas. It's about entrenching a culture inside the organisation that enables and provides permission for every person to participate in innovation.

The questions organisations and leaders need to be asking include:

- Are we focusing on our competencies for the future?

- Can we understand the signals from the market and customers that are indicators and precursors to disruption?

- Are we building a standardised culture for continuous forward thinking and innovation to get out of the innovation theatre and reward process?

- Are we populating our teams with risk-tolerant system thinkers who are able to uncover, prioritise, and solve the current and future problems of our customers?

- Are you encouraging your people to be pervasively curious?

- Are you humanising the process and removing the biases that are your greatest inhibitors?

The future of corporate innovation is one that isn't shackled to the theatre of innovation. There will be a distinction between the incremental programs and one that is an all-encompassing culture of seamless innovation and growth.

Innovation isn't a scientific formula. You can't hack this and find the cheats to get there faster. This is a culture that needs to build inside your organisation, and it's going to take time. If you continue to participate in innovation playing by rules that aren't meant for you, you're never going to find the success you aspire to. Change the game and understand you need to create new rules.

Surrender to the process and build the culture of Corporate Innervation that will transform your business.

Time is not on your side.

You'll wish you started yesterday.

Where to from here ...

We've come a long way, covered a lot of ground. It's been a wild ride through the good, the bad, and the ugly of all things corporate innovation.

We've gone all the way to the dark side with the inhibitors, biases, and myths that get in the way. I hope this has made you laugh, cringe a little, and provided you with some provocative questions for how you manage innovation with your people today. It's time to remove the startup, hustle culture and question everything.

I've shared a lot about my successes, processes, and a nine-step framework that you can start work on immediately inside your organisation. Use this to change the rules of the game for your organisation and embed a process and culture that will allow you to innovate differently and build success on your terms. Remember, you're not a startup.

I hope you take the time to reflect on and rethink innovation inside your organisation. Your people are your greatest asset, and they have the genius ideas that will make a difference to the organisation.

This is not something you get right overnight. Building and changing a culture takes time. Your brand, history, and current position in the market will mean nothing if you don't have the people internally to fulfill your strategic vision. This will take time, leadership, and dedication to build a human-centric innovation framework. This is more than just creating innovative products and solutions to make more money. This is about the longevity and culture of your organisation and making a solid return on your investment in innovation.

The rewards are worth it. Stick with it. Like I said, once you start to see the benefits, you'll wish you started yesterday.

About Ally Muller

Managing Director of GOYA Consulting, business owner, advisor, speaker, board member and enthusiastic researcher, known for providing commentary and advice on corporate innovation to ensure you are achieving results that will remove the theatre of innovation inside your organisation and deliver real bottom value.

Ally is an entrepreneurial professional with over 20 years strategy and management experience in corporate finance, infrastructure and technology-based companies, specialising in enterprise innovation strategy, business advisory, merger and acquisitions and board advisory.

With global experience delivering results for ASX 100, FTSE 100 and Fortune 50 companies, Ally has demonstrated success providing advice and leading transformation programs for innovation, strategy and new market development.

allymuller.com
goyaconsulting.com.au

Work with Ally Muller

If you have enjoyed reading *Corporate Innervation: Unlocking The Genius Inside Your Organisation*, there are a number of ways you can work with Ally Muller to rethink innovation and build a Corporate Innervation Operating System in your organisation.

Check out the information on the following pages or visit the websites:

allymuller.com
goyaconsulting.com.au

And of course you can also follow Ally on LinkedIn:

linkedin.com/in/allisonrmuller

Want to rethink your approach to innovation and implement the Corporate Innervation Operating System inside your organisation?

Work with Ally and the team at GOYA Consulting. We are problem-solvers, system thinkers, strategists, facilitators and implementers who bring a diverse range of experience to deliver amazing outcomes for our clients.

GOYA Consulting exists to help organisations deliver on their vision, goals and purpose. Strategising, problem-solving and enabling businesses to perform at their highest level is what makes us jump out of bed every day.

We're here to enable your vision.

We're here to simplify.

We have all the tools you need to succeed. No matter what stage you are at, we can support you to deliver value and increase the ability of your people to turn strategy and innovation into action.

If you would like to know more about working with GOYA Consulting get in touch with the team at hello@goyaconsulting.com.au

Work with Ally as a speaker for your next live or virtual event

Excite and inspire your audience to rethink innovation and build a culture of growth that delivers real benefits.

Ally delivers keynote presentations, masterclasses, workshops, webcasts and programs on business strategy and innovation. Ally shares her wisdom on how to think differently and expansively about innovation inside your organisation.

Passionate about innovation, strategic growth and empowering entrepreneurial cultures, Ally provides insights, experiences and the steps you need to take to build human-centric frameworks inside your organisation.

Ally will show you how to take those visionary ideas and make them a reality. She will take you on the journey of innovation to help you get more ideas, energise your teams and ultimately show you how to add real value to your bottom line. And she will do this in her straight-talking, personable way that will take you through the highs and lows of innovation and leave you with the ideas, processes and motivation to focus on making innovation work for the whole organisation. A great idea can only make an impact once it is implemented.

To find out more about getting Ally to speak at your next event, either face-to-face or virtually, contact the team at ally@allymuller.com or visit allymuller.com